Armed With A Football

Dedication

On my father's 75th and last birthday, in September 1992, I gave my parents a bound volume of this book. It was "for my parents". This edition, published in memory of Tim Ward (1917-1993), is for the Andrews family and my father's many friends.

Armed With A Football

A Memoir of Tim Ward, Footballer and Father

Andrew Ward

Crowberry

First Published in Great Britain by Crowberry, PO Box 623, Oxford, OX2 6DA, England.

ISBN 0 9507568 1 4

Designed and Typeset by Breedon Books, 44 Friar Gate, Derby, DE1 1DA, England.

Printed in Great Britain by Hillman Printers, Frome, Somerset.
Cover printed by BDC Printing Services Limited of Derby.

Contents

	Prologue	vii
	Acknowledgements	viii
1.	The FA Cup Final	1
2.	Our Heroes Worked on the Wing	10
3.	Meeting Raich Carter	21
4.	More Than Picking the Team	34
5.	Innocence Nil, Realism One	45
6.	Origins of a Football Family	62
7.	When Life Seemed as Fragile as a One-goal Lead	78
8.	Post-war Euphoria	97
9.	A Little Bit of Success in the League	117
10.	Football's Vera Lynns	132
11.	Homecoming Truths	144
	Postscript	150

Prologue

I spent my schooldays as a football manager's son. On Saturdays, during the season, I visited my father's workplace and watched and listened as thousands of people judged how well he had picked the team. It was a strong father-son bonding, secured by football's physicality, excitement and loyalty. As each season progressed, I shared my father's success and failure.

As a child, my father was my hero, football our obsession. Then, as I entered adulthood, life's experiences and higher education led me towards new worlds. Inevitably, in the Sixties and Seventies, my father and I differed, but we could always return to our sporting heritage. Around football we hung our understanding of life.

My father told me the kind of stories I had never read in books, so I began to write. I interviewed footballers from his managerial days at Barnsley in the Fifties, and began to view his life in a more rounded context. He was well-liked and respected but, like all managers, also hated by a few. He had weaknesses as well as strengths. I now saw him as Tim Ward rather than "Dad". The hero-worship diminished. I was left with family love.

My father's career continued to fascinate me. I delved into the years before 22 April 1949, the day that I was born. The more I learned of his past, the more he shared with me. Sometimes, when you explore a person beneath the surface, you encounter evasion, repetition or inaccuracy. My father, however, was always able to contribute a little bit more towards a coherent story. I grew to understand him. I needed to, because we were raised in such different eras. Through the Fifties and Sixties, I was protected by economic expansion, relative peace and a secure family unit, whereas he was a child of the Depression, uncertain about his family origins and, in his twenties, very lucky to survive a war. I grew to tolerate our differences, respect him again, and love him all the more.

When he died, at 9.55pm on Thursday 28 January 1993, his hand locked in mine, I felt his great strength and fighting spirit for the last time. For weeks football people had come to say their goodbyes, bringing dignity to his death. By then, my father and I had long since said those urgent, personal things that two people need to say when they know they might not see each other again. During our conversations, over the previous 20 years, he had told me everything a son could wish to know about a father's life. I had already completed this book. He trusted me with it and now I trust it with you.

Acknowledgements

Ian Alister, Anton Rippon, Karen MacDowell, Kevin McCarra, John Bright-Holmes, John Harding and Louise Dixon all read earlier drafts of the book and made very helpful comments that enabled me to discover more of the story and a better way of telling it. I am also grateful to the Andrews family, Mark Binnie, Canon Geoffrey Bird, Raich and Pat Carter and family, Cindy Caywood, Stuart Edwards, Barrie and Stella Haigh, Lisa Hammond, Coosje Hoogendoorn, Alf and Anna Jeffries, Alan Jenkins, Helen Kennerley, Mike and Annie Lean, Tim Leuty, Eugene MacBride, Gerald Mortimer, Jill Peay, Steve Redhead, Arne Richards, Rebecca Sawtell, Mrs Doris Walters, Evelyn Ward and Sue Wilkinson. I also received help from staff at the Imperial War Museum, the British Library Newspaper Library, the Football Association Library and Local Studies Libraries in Sheffield, Glasgow, Derby and Cheltenham. Special thanks are reserved for the following: Anton Rippon and the staff at Breedon Books for help with producing the book; Arne Richards, a supportive flatmate at a critical time in the project; Ian Alister, my co-publisher and co-author of *Barnsley: A Study in Football, 1953-59;* and Karen MacDowell, who provided encouragement and understanding. My greatest gratitude, of course, is to my parents.

1.
The FA Cup Final

As a football manager's son, I soon became aware of an event called "The FA Cup Final". The first one I remember was in 1955, when Newcastle United beat Manchester City soon after my sixth birthday. My father travelled to London to see the match, whereas I stayed at home to watch it with my mother on our new television set. I started to watch, but sitting still in a chair wasn't my forte. I saw a goal in the first minute and that was enough.

"I can do that," I thought, "I can score a goal like that."

I ran out into the back yard, threw my half-size ball at the wall and impersonated crosses from the Newcastle United right wing. As the ball rebounded, I raced to meet it and improvised with a flick of the head. Occasionally I fluked contact and sent the ball off in a similar direction to that conjured by Jackie Milburn at Wembley.

"Milburn scores for Newcastle United," I said, as the ball thudded against the garage doors and annoyed the neighbours. In that moment I believed I was Jackie Milburn. I would play for England soon. Like Jackie Milburn. Like my father.

A year later, in 1956, Manchester City returned to Wembley to beat Birmingham City, and Bert Trautmann, their heroic goalkeeper, completed the game with a broken neck. I spent the next week diving at everything in the house. I stopped the settee scoring when it was clear on goal and snatched the ball from the table leg when it tried to take the ball past me.

"You'll break your neck," my mother warned me.

I couldn't have asked for more.

My father was at Wembley to watch the 1957 Final and this time I settled to watching it on television. I wanted Manchester United to beat Aston Villa. One Manchester United player, Tommy Taylor, had played with my father at the club he now managed – Barnsley – and we felt close to another, Jackie Blanchflower, whose brother Danny had lived in our house before we did. In the Cup Final, Jackie Blanchflower spent most of the game as a deputy goalkeeper after Ray Wood had been injured in a challenge with Villa's Peter McParland. I also knew McParland really well – he was in my bubble-gum card collection.

My father and I watched the 1959 Final on television together. Nottingham Forest took a one-nil lead against Luton Town.

The telephone rang.

"Who could be ringing in the middle of the match?" my father asked.

He went out and talked on the telephone for a minute or two. How I loved that time. Not because Forest scored again. But because I felt responsible for remembering everything perfectly, to tell him when he came back.

"Any more score?"

"Yes, Dad. Nottingham Forest scored again. It's two-none. It was a long cross from the left wing and Tommy Wilson headed it into the other corner. The goalkeeper was rooted to the spot."

I felt very important.

I was helping him with his job.

Our family calendar registered seasons rather than years, and the climax to each season was the FA Cup Final. The event is still a great source of ritual, spectacle and drama, but, in our family, I also inherited a sense of the occasion's mystery. I was aware, from an early age, that my father had played professional football. I also knew that he had played for Derby County, and Derby County had won the FA Cup in 1946. Yet, even though my father was a regular first-team player from 1937 to 1951, he had not played in the 1946 FA Cup Final. His absence from the team that day baffled me for years, and others were baffled too. Some were convinced that he had played. Later in my life, researching this book, discovering how a top-class professional lived, worked, played and nearly died in the years around the Second World War, I realised why the 1946 Cup Final had left a puzzling legacy with me. It was, quite simply, because it had puzzled my father too.

1946

At 7am on the morning of the first post-war FA Cup Final, Tim Ward and his wife Nancy met an entourage of people with Derby County connections: players' wives and sweethearts, office staff and their spouses, gatemen, groundsmen and programme sellers. The entourage climbed into two coaches and set off for Harpenden. Lunch was on the club.

At Harpenden they met the Derby County players, and Tim came face-to-face with his strange circumstances.

For eight years he had considered himself to be a first-team player at Derby County. Now 28 years old, he was perfectly fit and playing better than ever. For the last few months he had been playing regularly, two games a week, against the best club sides in Britain or against European international teams. Derby County had always given him a game when he was available. If he wanted to play, he was in the team.

But not today.

Not for the Cup Final.

So he wondered why not.

After lunch, three Derby County coaches travelled in convoy to Wembley Stadium. The team's bus arrived at the players' entrance at about two o'clock. While Nancy Ward stayed outside, chatting to other players' wives amidst the backcloth of parked black cars and shouts of "Up Charlton" and "Good old Derby," Tim went inside. On the journey, he had promised himself a moment with the team in the dressing-room so he could say that he had been in a Wembley dressing-room. Derby County were in Wembley's best dressing-room – they had won the toss – but Tim wasn't especially impressed. He had been more affected by his first visits to dressing-rooms at Highbury, Villa Park, Goodison Park or even the Baseball Ground, home of Derby County. Of course, he had also been more impressionable nine years ago when a country boy accustomed to Cheltenham Town's Whaddon Road.

Tim went back outside, found Nancy, and escorted her through entrance G75 to their seats. He paid sixpence for a match programme which showed evidence of wartime austerity. The only substantial reading was two double-page spreads of pen pictures, written by Roy Peskett of the *Daily Mail.* It did, however, inform spectators what was happening. When Tim and Nancy reached their seats, the Band of the Grenadier Guards was playing.

As kick-off approached, the crowd sang better and better.

"And now," said the Director of Music, conducting spectators from his podium. "And now for number 15 on your song-sheet."

Nearly a hundred thousand voices entered the verses of the hymn. They sang an extra verse and concluded with the chorus:

Abide with me; fast falls the eventide;

They sang with belief and respect. They were all moved. They thanked some untouchable force for keeping them alive during the last seven years.

The darkness deepens; Lord with me abide

They were grateful that normality was restored. Wasn't this the first Cup Final for seven years? Wasn't it a sign that things were back to normal?

When other helpers fail, and comforts flee

Spectators sang slowly and softly, and devoured every word. Singing in the streets was now transferred to singing at Wembley. Whatever the result, it was a celebration of victory for both sides.

Help of the helpless, O abide with me.

Caps and hats were taken off, inhibitions discarded, and many began to weep.

He sat on a bench-seat (row 32 seat 143) in the open air of the North Terrace at Wembley Stadium, waiting for the match to begin. Derby County were playing, and Derby County were his team. Oh, more than that. Derby County were his first love, his employer, his whole reason for being. He should have been delighted at sitting in a free seat (and not a bad view) on such an important occasion, but something disturbed him immensely: he craved to be on the pitch.

He leaned forward in his seat and tried to conceal his disappointment with integrity. He did, after all, want Derby County to win.

The players came out of the tunnel and were greeted by a roar. Tim knew all the Derby County players and most of Charlton Athletic's. He knew little things that supporters didn't. He knew his friend Leon would be last out, according to superstition, and would be wearing knee bandages. Tim had known Leon go back to the dressing-room for a knee bandage if he had come out without it by mistake. On the pitch Leon would be known as "Lee".

The crowd waited for King George VI.

A delay added to the stress. The players were keyed up, desperate to kick a football, and yet minutes went by as they waited. Tim could sense that Raich Carter was growing impatient. Raich broke from the line of Derby County players and walked around. Tim wondered what he would be doing if he was in the line with them.

Finally, after five minutes' wait, the King was seen walking towards the pitch. His grey overcoat gave him the look of a civilian.

"Blimey, he's been demobbed too," a spectator shouted through the cheering.

Then the spectators were respectfully silent as the band struck up the first notes of "God Save the King". The King stopped at the touch-line, and the crowd sang as though God had saved the country.

When the national anthem was over, the King was led forward to meet the players. The King was introduced to Derby captain Jack Nicholas.

"Probably the hardest handshake the King's had this year," somebody said.

Tim knew 'Nick' as well as any player in the line. He had played enough times with the rough, tough Derby captain. He watched Jack Nicholas introduce the Derby players to the King, and kept his eyes on them while the King walked across to the men of Charlton Athletic.

The players were polite and dignified. Their hair was uniformly cropped short, in some cases level with the top of their ears at the back. They wore long shorts, almost knee length, and boots taped with sticking plaster. Some boots were more white tape than brown leather.

Tim's feelings of exclusion intensified as players trotted to respective ends to warm nervous muscles. Watching did not come easily to him. He preferred to kick a ball himself. He always wanted to be involved, whether it be a kickaround game or something more organised.

"Derby's gone up the wrong end," said a former Derby County player sitting on Tim's left. "When I was here with Newcastle we went up the other end and we won."

"All I need is a pessimist next to me," Tim thought. He was becoming irritated, frustrated at being in the grandstand, wanting the game to begin. Such was the lottery of ticket allocation that neighbours were unpredictable, except for his wife, Nancy, who sat to his right. But among nearly 100,000 others, Tim suddenly felt lonely in the crowd. The ideal number for him was twenty-one others, plus a referee and two linesmen. That was true belonging.

He gazed distantly, towards the basic dress of the Derby County players: white shirts, black shorts and black socks with white tops. The socks looked more suited to referees than players. Despite the uniform clothing of the players, he had no trouble distinguishing them without looking at the numbers on the back of their shirts. That muscular run of Jack Stamps, the odd pin-toed ramble of Dally Duncan, the unmistakable grey-haired bounce of Raich Carter and the imminent energy of the red-haired Peter Doherty. Even in the warm-up kicks, he saw enough to feel confident that his team would win.

"Why aren't you playing?"

"Have you been away at the war?"

"You should be out there."

Nancy Ward turned round and looked at a man who sported a black-and-white rosette that must have been a foot in diameter. It blared news of the man's support for Derby County – "Up the Rams" – and had a small tinsel replica of the FA Cup trophy. No onlooker could doubt the man's loyalties. He was ablaze with black and white. And even though it was a warm day he wore a scarf conveying the names of Derby players – a black "Woodley" on a white background, a white "Nicholas" on a black background, and so on.

Still turning round, Nancy let her eyes stray to other supporters in the stand. She saw the black-and-white bowler hats and trilbies, and felt happy to be part of the scene.

The man with the black-and-white scarf gave a twirl of his black-and-white rattle and a peculiar noise resonated around Nancy's ears.

"Come on the Raaaaaaaaams!"

Should Tim be out there? He was beginning to believe it. Who were those Derby County players down there? Most of them had never played a Football League game for Derby County and yet were about to play a Cup Final at Wembley. The goalkeeper had been raked out of retirement for two semi-final games and a Cup Final. He was barely a Derby County player. Nobody could say that about Tim.

Bubbling beneath the surface was anger and confusion. He wasn't even injured or short of match practice. He had done nothing wrong. Before the war he had been first-choice wing-half in a good Derby County team, a Championship-class team. Now he was much more experienced, confident, and even more accustomed to playing with international-class players. "Surely," he thought, "my body is in better condition than ever. What kind of a hero's return is this? What kind of fair treatment of soldiers?"

He fought his anger. The team must come first, he argued. He must not show he was hurt. Or so he believed.

Nancy was more fatalistic. "It's just your luck," she would say.

Yes, and it could be worse. He could be dead. He was very aware of that.

He also realised that several other absent Derby County players had better claims than him, especially the recently injured. Look at Sammy Crooks. Sammy was fit again. Sammy had played through the Cup rounds. Sammy had given Derby County everything in a career of nearly 20 years and had been England's outside-right for most of the 1930s, but he wasn't playing today. Tim felt a long way behind

Sammy when Cup Final places were being awarded, and he knew Sammy's good humour wasn't affected. The mere thought of Sammy Crooks was enough to quell Tim's anger. He settled down to watch the 1946 Cup Final quietly.

"Come on the Rams," he thought to himself. "Come on the Rams."

A new wave of excitement was created as the two captains shook hands. Don Welsh and Jack Nicholas were men of the same generation, their features made craggy by their trade. The referee took a coin from his blazer and tossed it high. Don Welsh guessed the spin correctly and asked the teams to switch halves. As the players crossed over and greeted each other, the ball waited on its central spot. There was no turning back. After wartime years of deprivation, everybody in the stadium wanted to go forward. All the hard work was done. Play would begin.

The task of initiating the action, reacting to the sound of the referee's whistle and turning eager anticipation into real concentration, fell to Jack Stamps, the Derby County centre-forward. His simple foot-to-ball movement started a million other motions, and the watching Tim Ward was already engrossed.

Nancy looked 25 yards to her left and studied dignitaries in the Royal Box. It was the closest she had ever been to King George VI, and that in itself was enough to make this day one of the nicest of her life. The King, smoking a cigarette, sat next to the Queen. The Mayor of Derby, dressed in his red robes of office, sat between the King and Princess Elizabeth. "What a wonderful thing for Derby," Nancy thought. "Our Mayor surrounded by royalty." She let her eyes linger on the Royal Box long enough to identify the Earl of Athlone from his picture in the programme, then she was pulled back to watching the game by the collective power of what was happening around her.

In the first few minutes Jack Nicholas charged his Charlton opponent with the full weight of his hefty shoulder. No one went past Jack Nicholas without a permit or a getaway car. The Derby man met the Scottish winger shoulder to shoulder, the ball in playing distance, so it was perfectly fair. It signified that a match was on.

There are many ways to describe a football match. Announcers do it by the score – Charlton Athletic one, Derby County four. Others like statistics – 83 throw-ins, 35 free-kicks, five goals and one winning team. Some prefer to log unusual incidents, like the saga of the dog. A Charlton player spotted it first. He talked to it, knelt near it, attracted its friendly attention and stroked it before leading it away by the collar.

Others remember a match by a remark. During the half-time interval, 40 men from the Army Physical Training Corps came on the field wearing white gymnastic gear. They vaulted over boxes and entertained the crowd.

"They're more athletic than the players," somebody joked.

Some people like the debate. The 1946 Cup Final remained exciting and goalless until the last 10 minutes of the game, when one of Wembley's most unusual minute's play occurred.

A goal for Derby County was swiftly followed by a Charlton Athletic equaliser.

But who scored the goals?

How did the ball go in?

Spectators around Tim tried to agree on the goalscorers. Tim's opinion was respected more than most. Some were celebrating the Derby goal and missed the Charlton equaliser.

"Was it an own-goal?"

"Were they both own-goals?"

"Dally Duncan, wasn't it?"

"Didn't theirs hit someone in the wall."

One-one, and the same man, Bert Turner of Charlton, had scored both goals, although Tim and others were willing to debate it.

Another odd incident came near the end. Jack Stamps shot, the ball burst and Charlton goalkeeper Sam Bartram caught it. Sam, realising what had happened, threw the punctured ball towards the touch-line, towards a safer place for the referee to drop a new ball. It took an age to find another ball, then two minutes to complete the match as a draw.

"It would happen to Sam," Tim thought. "Things always happened to Sam." Other players forever told Tim stories about Sam. How the goalkeeper would run out to head the ball or kick it into touch. Or about the time he took a penalty and unintentionally lofted the ball over the crossbar as if it were a goal-kick. Or a story about a game in the late 1930s that was abandoned through fog. The players had been in the bath for 10 minutes and Sam was still jumping around his penalty area, thinking his team were doing a lot of attacking.

And now a burst ball in an FA Cup Final.

There had been a spate of burst balls. These balls weren't as good as the pre-war ones. Good materials weren't as available.

Tim realised how lucky he had been. He had survived the war. He had been equipped with a good football.

Extra-time for the same price. An encore to thrill the audience. Spectators around Tim read aloud the note in the programme: "Should the match result in a draw after 90 minutes play, an extra half hour will be played." The first post-war Cup Final went to extra-time and an extra ball.

It promised a lot. The first 90 minutes had started slowly and ended with a rousing fanfare.

Tim had so far watched the game with utter concentration. He felt Derby County were favourites now. Raich Carter knew the pattern of play and Peter Doherty had unlimited stamina. The two wing-halves, Jimmy Bullions and Chick Musson, were playing the games of their lives. But Tim didn't know where that left his own career. Wing-half was his position.

Leon Leuty was perhaps the best of them all. At centre-half, he covered the breadth of the field, heading clearances to men on the touch-lines, passing to Carter and Doherty with relentless accuracy. Growing taller by the minute, Leon was the good-looking actor who knew all his lines, and the knee bandages simply added to the heroism. He was possibly the most handsome man in football, and showed his relaxed big-match manner, totally unrattled, cool and confident. His speed of recovery was remarkable, his tackling belied his seemingly frail physique. His technique showed the precision of a toolmaker who had served his apprenticeship. Tim felt proud that Leon was his friend.

Play began again. Tim and Nancy Ward edged forward on their five-shilling bench-seats, and a goal was quickly scored. Jack Stamps went clear on the left wing and crossed the ball into the penalty area. Dally Duncan and Peter Doherty, running like trains on converging tracks, looked as though they would collide. Peter called that he was better-placed for the shot. He stroked the ball into the net with his left foot and later that claimed that he, not Bert Turner, had scored at both ends.

Derby County fans celebrated as much as they could. Caps and hats were thrown so high that supporters never retrieved them. Programmes and song-sheets were waved as for a ticker-tape welcome, and the rest of the game was a celebration. As the 100th minute went by, and older Charlton players tired, Derby centre-forward Jack Stamps imposed his strength and stamina on the outcome. He scored the third Derby County goal, receiving the ball after Doherty had treated it to a few dazzling flicks, then steering it past Sam Bartram's right hand with his left foot. Then he added a fourth.

For Derbians it was compulsive, total release after the black-out days of the war. It was their team, their town, their Cup. The war may (or may not) have been won on Rolls-Royce engines, but the Cup had been won by a couple of Rolls-Royce inside-forwards, overshadowed at the end by a work-a-day centre-forward called Jack Stamps. But cliché demands that it was the work of a team, and the names of the team would become as important to Derby children of the era as multiplication tables or the alphabet.

Jack Nicholas led the players towards the Royal Box. He collected the Cup from the King, and gave a speech in front of the Movietone News cameras: "Well, I'm very pleased to be taking this trophy back to Derby for the first time in history, and I'm very proud to be the captain of the side that's done it."

As the players lapped in honour, they were joined by other people, including manager Stuart McMillan, who was typically dapper in suit, gloves and striped tie. Carrying his trilby hat, his immaculate dark hair exposed, McMillan looked quite a toff.

Tim watched it all from the stand.

In the dressing-room they toasted with ginger-beer. Champagne was rationed, even ginger-beer wasn't easy to get, but the atmosphere was enough to inebriate the Derby County players.

Tim threaded through the crowd to join them.

Leon sat in the dressing-room with memories flooding back. He recalled those who had helped him recover from two cartilage operations, people like Notts County manager Frank Womack and his colleagues at Rolls Royce. He thought about his greatest fan.

"I think I'll give my medal to my mother to take home," Leon said to no one in particular.

If you're not part of the team, you're not part of the scene. It's a feeling as old as the Shrovetide game, and Tim, delighted though he was, was not part of the team.

He hung around the dressing-room and collected autographs in the centre page of his match programme.

On the Sunday the Derby players bought newspapers. Lots of them. They talked about scrapbooks and read aloud the pieces they fancied reading to themselves in years to come. That evening they took the FA Cup to a St Albans cinema, where they saw a newsreel film of the Cup Final. Three of the players took the trophy on a visit to one of Jack Nicholas's relatives in Staines. They had a drink in the Blue Anchor.

Tim quickly became part of the team again. He stayed with the other players in the Gleneagles Hotel, and was told he would play at Southampton on the Monday night. He had missed only one game.

2.
Our Heroes Worked on the Wing

I vaguely remember watching Barnsley play Chester soon after my sixth birthday. The crowd came on the pitch at the end and everyone celebrated. Or maybe my memory has played a trick. Perhaps I have only seen photographs in an unsolicited scrapbook, sent to my father by a supporter called David H Brown. As a child I coveted that scrapbook and read it hundreds of times. David H Brown had saved reports and photographs from all except one of Barnsley's 49 League and Cup games that season. I read them all. Again and again. I studied the headlines – "Quick Brace puts Reds on Top," "Tranmere 'Aunt Sally' for Barnsley" – and devoured the text. I witnessed things I hadn't really seen.

When I did watch games, I sat high in the Main Stand at Barnsley, my mother at my side, my father some distance away, hidden in the dug-out on our side of the pitch. I saw him approach the players' tunnel at half-time and saw him again at the end. Once he bobbed up from the dug-out to catch the ball and throw it back. Someone near me said "his team" were playing. I didn't know what it meant.

When I was seven I fell into idolism with a gentle left winger called John McCann. I had other favourites, but Johnny McCann had been signed by my father for only £500 from a Scottish Junior team called Bridgeton Waverley. Our new left winger soon created a stir in the Second Division. They said he was really worth £20,000 and was a future international. I was proud of my father for signing him.

John McCann preferred the ball at his feet rather than risk the physical contact that followed throughballs. I loved it when he deftly flicked the ball over the clumsy, sliding legs of a ruthless full-back, his own legs skipping daintily to avoid the carnage. Or when he clipped in high crosses to my other heroes. And especially when he hit hard, low crosses in the hope of a slight deflection from friend or foe. My father told me this was intelligent football, so I believed it was.

Football's foreplay came in many forms. It could be the initial lunge of a sliding-tackle, a leap to head the ball, an attacker's turn towards goal, a corner-kick or a player shaping to shoot. All promised something more. But I reacted most when the ball was next to Johnny McCann's left foot. I waited for him to do something exciting. I was convinced that Johnny's left foot could thread a football through the eye of a needle and land it on a seal's nose.

With Johnny McCann, I stood in front of wing-halves from Nottingham Forest and Liverpool when they took throw-ins. With Johnny McCann, I took the ball on my chest and let it drop gently to my feet. With Johnny McCann, I danced and jigged with defenders before coming away with the ball. With Johnny McCann, I dribbled towards the corner-flag and then became confused as spectators stood up in front of me and blocked my view.

Thanks to my hero, though, I learned the meaning of some of my father's expressions.

"Johnny McCann went past the full-back as if he wasn't there."

"Johnny McCann took them apart."

"Johnny McCann went crazy against the Bristol City right-back."

"Johnny McCann's an intelligent player."

I grew up in an era when wingers were the stars. They worked the touch-line and entertained us with their flicks and follies. They were our nearest football-kitted friends, close enough to establish a real relationship with us. We could talk to them, and they listened.

"Take him on."

"Leave him for dead."

We didn't see much of Stan Matthews or Tom Finney at Barnsley in the 1950s, but I didn't feel deprived. I could watch top-class wingers like Johnny McCann and outside-right Arthur Kaye, and I knew that my father was on good terms with the best wingers England had ever produced. He had played for England with Finney and Matthews, who were on our Christmas-card list – a privileged way to begin an autograph collection. And wasn't there some talk of a famous inter-war England international called Sammy Crooks?

1930

At first light on Saturday morning, as a child, Tim woke up with an anticipation that sent waves of energy through his body. It was always a good day if he played sport at least once, but Saturdays were different. Whole Saturdays were spent on sport, from dawn to dusk, whatever the weather.

He leapt off the canopy bed and seriously considered hanging from the bedroom window and jumping the reasonably short distance to the ground. Instead he ran downstairs, gobbled his breakfast and then set off to see if Cedric was coming out to play. Tim walked out past the front garden, past the bushes that gave the house its name ("The Briars") – how he hated fighting the prickles to recover tennis balls – and turned down London Road towards his friend's house. It was only a 50-yard journey. Cedric lived four doors away.

He knocked hard on Cedric's door and threw stones at the window. This was always a tense moment. Sometimes Cedric's asthma was so bad that he couldn't play and Tim would stand edgily on the doorstep, wondering if he dare ask to borrow Cedric's leather football. To play with a real football was a special part of the week, and Tim and Cedric had a deal. Tim agreed to go to church on Sundays – Cedric's father was parish clerk – and Cedric let Tim play with his real football on Saturdays. But Tim usually tried to play football on Sundays, too, even though Sunday sport was taboo and anyone caught playing would be threatened with fire and damnation by the vicar's foghorn voice.

"Is Cedric coming out to play?"

"Just a minute, Tim."

When Cedric appeared he put Tim to shame. He always did. Cedric's mother ran a laundry, so Cedric's kit was always immaculate when he left his house. It was always beautifully laundered, even if it had been worn for only a few minutes.

"I'll be Arsenal," said Cedric, when he came to the door. Wearing his sparkling kit, carrying his real football under his arm, Cedric was in a different class. He deserved to be top of the First Division. He deserved to be the Arsenal, even though he wore a white shirt and not Arsenal's red.

The two boys walked on to London Road and felt comforted by the smells. The fragrance of dripping-cakes from Mills' Bakery had replaced last night's stench of Sabettelini's fish and chips. Sabattelini was an Italian who sold ice-cream in the summer and fish and chips in the winter. The district could smell him coming in winter and, as his tired horse plodded up the hill, mothers assessed orders and small boys collected a week's newspapers from neighbours so the Italian would offer them a free penny-worth of chips.

A Harley-Davidson motor bike started up across the way. People stood at gates and chatted. These days you didn't know whether they were being friendly or were minding gates and fences that could be stolen for firewood by the less fortunate. The boys walked to the fields. Sometimes they played on the ridge-and-furrow surface of the Beeches, but this time they played on Fox Fields, keeping one eye out for the farmer. Cedric and Tim competed one-to-one – the Arsenal against Tim. But this Arsenal team consisted only of one asthmatic boy and the opposition was a determined stamina-freak who played for Cheltenham Schoolboys. The contest was in Tim's favour. Cedric's main advantages were his professional appearance and the realisation that he could fall over in mud and escape a haranguing from home as his kit would always be professionally cleaned later. Generally it was not enough. Tim latched on to the real football and dribbled energetically and persistently towards the Arsenal goal, and anybody watching from a distance, walking a dog or cutting across Fox Fields, might think that each of Tim's goals was the England winner over Scotland rather than an extra goal to add to a comfortable victory.

Every Saturday he played fervently to win and every Saturday he beat Cedric. But he was never fully satisfied by victory, for Cedric was still the Arsenal, and the Arsenal were still the best. From their north London base, about 90 miles from Cheltenham, somewhere at the end of the road on which Tim and Cedric lived, Arsenal had assembled a team which started the 1930-31 football season with a clinical destruction that hinted of invincibility. Six weeks into the season, the FA Cup holders were unbeaten. No one could beat them, certainly not a Charlton Kings teenager. Then, one Saturday, Tim found a way to loosen the hold that Cedric's

Arsenal had over him. He fell in love with a football team that beat the Arsenal, and he was on his way to discovering a hero.

Tim read the *Sunday Pictorial* avidly for word of football competition, and he learned of Arsenal's 4-2 defeat at Derby County. Before long he had added a touch of detail. Tim pictured himself as an outside-right, a position he had played for Cheltenham Boys, and the Derby County outside-right was called Crooks, a distant, untouchable professional who now began to occupy a fragment of Tim's imagination: Who is this Crooks? He read what he could and learned that Sammy Crooks was an England international outside-right, fast, clever with the ball, difficult for opponents to mark. And so he discovered an idol to defend if things went wrong, to praise when they went well. Sammy Crooks played for Derby County, and Derby County had beaten the Arsenal.

"I'll be Arsenal," said Cedric, the next time they played.

But now Tim had a reply.

"I'll be Derby County," he said.

And so a club came into his life, a team with simple kit, no more colourful than the photographs of the day, for Derby County players wore white shirts and black shorts. Tim could not copy that, but he could pretend. If Cedric was Arsenal in a white shirt, Tim could be Derby County in a shirt of any colour. So, whatever he wore, he was Derby County, and, thereafter, when he beat Cedric on Fox Fields or the Beeches, his victory was more complete.

It was safe playing with Cedric, much safer than playing with older boys, but Tim never shirked. Ever since he was eight or nine, he had joined in with boys as old as sixteen, compensating for his lack of size and strength with energy and determination, developing tricks with the ball to keep himself from too much trouble. He grew doubly determined and trebly tenacious. He was playing so hard, so well, that they had to let him play, and he always wanted to win, to topple the Arsenals he met in the streets and on the fields. At times, he became fierce and mad as his determination bubbled over. And when that happened, or when Tim was winning, the losers among the older boys would respond.

In Tim's case there was an easy taunt, an obvious black mark against his name, as viewed by some in the community. He kept quiet about it as much as possible, but he couldn't change his name. Other children knew he had a different surname from his brothers. It was easy to exact revenge when playing football.

One day the taunts grew too strong.

"They'll come and take you back," one boy said when the football game became emotional.

"They'll take you away," said another.

Tim didn't want to go anywhere. Nor did he want to slow down and give in, so he ran from the taunts. He ran with determination, as fast as he could, towards the nearby hills, hills omnipresent to Charlton Kings, easily spotted in the near distance peeping through gaps between houses, some hills with a thin line of trees, others thickly forested. He ran towards the outline of the Devil's Chimney, a peculiar, spectacular stone monument which offered a panoramic view of Cheltenham. Up there the background peace and quiet was punctuated only by bird calls, a dog in the distance and scurrying rabbits. If he saw people, searching the countryside for food or hunting along the railway-line for coal dropped from a train, he ran away from them too. He ran and ran and ran.

When he had recovered from his run, when he had drawn his breath, he listened closely and heard the delayed sounds of children kicking a football. And when he heard the echo-like sound of foot on ball, he conceded that that was where he belonged, that was where he wanted to be. It always felt good to run, the hills improved his stamina and security, but once there, once rested, he vowed to come down and outkick and outrun the other boys. He would become another Sammy Crooks and play on the right wing for Derby County and England. He would help Derby County win the League Championship, unseating this famous, much-mentioned club called Arsenal, and he would help Derby County win the FA Cup. He could imagine wireless broadcasters commentating on the FA Cup Final and the whole nation hearing the words: "It's Ward again, by jove… square three… moving into the Arsenal half… square five… he's running along the right wing… square seven… moving inside… square seven… he shoots and it's a goal. Derby County have won the Cup."

And when Tim had taken in the vista of Cheltenham and played out his dreams and recovered from his uphill run, he reassured himself that he was still part of a family, even if they were called Andrews rather than Ward, and he was glad of it. He set off down the hill, even more determined to show the other boys what he could do. He knew that he made other boys mad because he was a good player, and that did not bother him. That would not stop him from playing. Instead, it was a reason to play as much as he dared and as well as he could.

1931

"Sir, what are we going to see?"

"West Bromwich Albion against Sheffield Wednesday," the teacher announced.

It was Tim's first view of a Football League game. He was thirteen, very close to fourteen, captain of Cheltenham Boys and playing regularly at centre-forward. As captain he normally made his own decision on which way to play if he won the toss, never bothering about the sun or the wind, just playing the way he liked. Every year Cheltenham Boys made a short-lived challenge for the English Shield trophy, and that involved a lengthy trip if the game was away. This was such an occasion.

For Cheltenham schoolchildren, the world of professional soccer was a different planet. It was almost unthinkable to travel 30 miles to Swindon, home of the nearest Football League club, and it was further still to Birmingham and Bristol. Besides, the Cheltenham hinterland was a depressing region for professional football. The two Bristol clubs were unsuccessful, their supporters talking of relegation or re-election, while Wiltshire's Swindon Town were an ordinary Division Three South team. Nearby Worcestershire had no Football League club.

So Tim was fortunate, at a time of growing unemployment, to be given the treat of a First Division Football League match. And these were top-class teams: FA Cup holders West Brom against Sheffield Wednesday, League Champions just over a year ago.

Tim had seen adult games before. He had watched his local amateur teams, Charlton Kings and Charlton St Mary's, and had seen Southern League Cheltenham Town a couple of times. But this was different. This was a rite of passage, a barmitzvah of the sporting religion. This was the largest crowd Tim had ever seen, buzzing with its collective enthusiasm and excitement. This was an introduction to the First Division of the Football League and first-hand knowledge of how twenty-two clubs competed, week-in, week-out, from August to May.

In the Hawthorns grandstand at West Bromwich, Tim sat in a line of Cheltenham Boys' players, and together they perceived professional footballers as men who came down from mountains. He felt the stir of high-level competition, heard the crescendo of noise as the first place-kick of the match was taken, and listened to strange, nasal voices suggesting that teams could beat the Arsenal and win the best competition in the world – the Football League Championship. Tim did not dare ask questions but he observed and listened. He took it all in.

He bought a souvenir that day. It was a handkerchief, a white handkerchief, with a printed team photograph of the West Bromwich players who had won the Cup at Wembley. Tim showed the handkerchief and its picture to everyone he knew in Cheltenham. He loved his souvenir and it was never out of his sight. The handkerchief was soon filthy and went in with the rest of his laundry.

When the handkerchief came out of the wash, it was plain white. The picture had gone.

1935

There was a stamp of perfection on the setting for the pre-season practice-match. The hard ground was covered by an unusually uniform green grass on Cheltenham Town's Whaddon Road pitch. Cheltonians talked optimistically about the season ahead. They knew what to expect from the pre-season ritual – the Southern League first-teamers ("the Red-and-Whites") against the Birmingham Combination reserve team ("the Blues"). As players took over the dressing-rooms and began to change, Tim mingled with them uncomfortably.

He had been training with Cheltenham Town for part of the previous season. Now seventeen, his height was average for his age, but he was very slightly built, too frail to be pitched into senior competitive soccer, in the judgment of Cheltenham Town manager George Carr.

Tim stood around, fidgeted and tried to look inconspicuous. Shortly before kick-off an agitated trainer approached him.

"Get changed, son," the trainer said. "Outside-right for the reserves. Blue shirt. The winger hasn't turned up. Hurry up, lad."

Tim broke his own unofficial fast-change record. He had read of players' careers starting when a player failed to turn up. Here was a chance, in a familiar outside-right position, one of only two positions he had played for his school team and Cheltenham Schoolboys. He could be a hero. Just like Sammy Crooks.

He was ready just in time to tag on to the blue-shirted crocodile that filed on to the pitch. They were shepherded towards an old school bench. A man perched with a tripod and camera six yards away.

"Can we have five of you on the form," the photographer shouted. "Forwards at the front on the bench. Defenders standing at the back."

Tim tried to work it out. He was a forward. He sat at the end at the front. The pressure from the big men next to him came against his left side. He could barely hold his position.

A photographer took pictures and Tim thought about what it all meant. His friends could see him in the *Gloucestershire Echo* on Monday. Playing for Cheltenham Town. He was proud.

A few minutes later the players took their positions for the place-kick which started the match. Tim selected a patch of ground on the right wing. His concentration on the scene was so intense, his stomach so uneasy, that he almost didn't hear the trainer shouting at him.

"Come on, son," the trainer yelled. "It's alright, son. Hackett's here. You can come off."

Tim pointed to his chest.

"Yeah," the trainer assented. "Hurry up off the pitch. Let's have your shirt."

The youngster came off the pitch. He stood and watched his team compete with ten men until Hackett took the place he had not quite had.

He would never forget his début for Cheltenham Town Reserves, if that's what it could be called.

On Boxing Day the Cheltenham Town reserve team travelled north for one of three games in four days. Jackie Simmons had news for them when he squeezed into one of the two hired cars at Redditch.

"We're playing at Villa Park, lads."

"How do you know?"

"They've just telephoned through to our pub."

"Wow," Tim thought. "Villa Park. The Villa Park. Where Aston Villa's first team played. Where top games are played. Where Derby County and Sammy Crooks have played."

Most of Cheltenham Town's reserve players had heard of Villa Park. Heard of it, but never visited. When they arrived they were staggered by the size of the dressing-rooms – big enough for a dinner-dance – and overwhelmed by the news of their opponents.

"That Talbot's playing," one said.

"Isn't he an international?"

"I dunno."

"Their reserve game's off. They've got their reserve team out."

After the match, won easily by Villa (four-one), Tim lay soaking in one of Villa's special slipper-baths. He could remember taking throw-ins during the game, but could recall no other contribution on a heavy, well-used pitch which stank of mud. A team-mate walked across.

"Well, young un, how did you enjoy playing your first match on Villa Park?"

"I'm not sure I played in it," Tim said. He couldn't remember having a kick.

As his team-mate laughed, Tim continued to mull. If he ever returned to Villa Park, if he did get a second chance, he would make sure he had a kick.

1936

He played with energy and impulse. That's how it began. He was raw and competitive, and subtlety and anticipation were words in someone else's dictionary. He ran after the ball, harried players far bigger than him, and, when he had the ball at his feet, he moved it quickly or, when his confidence was higher, tried to beat as many players as possible, just as he had as a schoolboy. Switched to wing-half, defensive duties were a new dimension. At first, when colleagues asked him who he was marking, he pointed to the winger. Eventually he was told directly: "Don't watch the winger. Watch the inside man."

By the time he played against Birmingham Trams, after three months in an unbeaten side, he had added a twinge of sophistication to his wing-half play. His throw-ins were less risky and more accurate, his tackles were stronger, and he sensed that he must compensate for lack of brawn with timing, technique and determination. He cleared the ball quickly inside his own penalty area, and, inside the worn central rhombus of the pitch, he confidently tricked players with skilful footwork before sending the ball ahead for the winger to take in his stride.

And then came something else.

He kicked a long forward pass and watched with surprise as the ball struck an invisible trampoline outside the penalty area defended by the Birmingham Trams team. The ball rose outrageously over the goalkeeper's elongated body and dropped neatly into the net. His team-mates laughed, shrugged their shoulders, shook his hand, and Tim learned something new. A goal is a goal is a goal, no matter how it is scored.

1937

Saturday was always the best day of Tim's week, especially when he became a regular choice for the Cheltenham Town first team. He loved the novel Saturday rituals of huddling around the gas fire, holding a mug of hot tea at half-time, the mug too big, the tea too hot to drink in the 10-minute interval. He loved fitting in with a team of older men, pampering their superstitions. He needed one for himself, something to give Saturday even more importance, something to ritualise the match.

On his Southern League début, against Newport County Reserves, his team won four-three and Tim made one goal with a shot that hit the crossbar and then scored another, experiencing the joy of having his arm pumped as if his team-mates were bringing water from a well.

The Cheltenham Town ground was his home ground and much more. He had played such a lot of football in the Whaddon Road area of Cheltenham – first on the recreation ground across the road, now on the grown-ups' famous pitch. The ground was uncovered at both ends but a stand ran along one side. The manager sat in the open air, unless it rained (when he crouched under the stand instead). It was nothing elaborate, but that flimsy stand and the advertising hoardings – SHARPS & FISHER, E.L.WARD – were enough to convince Tim that he was playing at Wembley. And if he looked past the corner-flag at the country-end of the ground, he could see his favourite hills grinning at him over the roofs of the houses of Whaddon Road. He really was playing at home.

And then a scout saw a game, and enjoyed what he saw.

He left home on a Monday in March, walking three miles through the streets of Cheltenham to the railway station, carrying a small leather case. He took no sandwiches and no expectations. He didn't know where Derby was or what it would be like.

It was not the first time he had travelled: his father had taken the whole family to Weymouth; he'd been on Sunday School outings to a place they called "Weston-super-Mud"; and Cheltenham Town had played as far away as Folkestone. But this was different. This was alone. This was leaving home.

The train seemed to travel all day. It stopped at stations with names he did not know.

"Is this Durby," he asked at last.

"No, it's Darby."

He decided to get off anyway. He was met on the platform by Bill Bromage, one of the Derby County trainers, a round-faced man with hair swept forward. Bromage wore a big polo-necked jumper under a three-piece suit, and a watch-chain hung from the front of his waistcoat. He took Tim to digs in Normanton and left him with a homely, friendly widow called Mrs Smith, a landlady accustomed to bemothering footballers and policemen.

Then, in his room, he was alone again, wondering: "Where are the orchards and hills? Why can I no longer hear chickens and ducks and pigs? Who has stolen the fields for playing football?"

Early that evening he went to the pictures. It was dark when he came out of the Normanton cinema, and he was soon lost. His five-minute walk turned into something more. He ambled aimlessly along streets of red-brick terrace houses, searching for a familiar name. Eventually he saw it – Crewe Street. And the number? Was it two-oh-six? It was some time before he was confident enough to knock on the door of his new home.

He was lying in bed, awake, wondering whether to cry, when his room-mate came in from a late cinema show in town. Alf went to the window, looked out and called to the next room: "Hey, Sid, they're here again."

Suddenly the window was open and two young footballers were serenading a courting couple across the street.

Good-night, Sweet-heart
All my pray'rs are for you,
Good-night, Sweet-heart
I'll be watching o'er you

They sang the song all the way through, and Tim began to smile. "What a madhouse," he thought. For the first time he was experiencing the camaraderie of Derby County footballers. His sense of belonging was back. He already knew he faced plenty of hard work. Now he knew that what lay ahead could also be a lot of fun.

In his second week working for Derby County he met a first-team player. Tim came out of the away-team dressing-room – used by lower-team players – and walked along the passage in training kit, ready to run on to the field. The door of the first-team changing-room opened. A man came out, bright-eyed with swept-back hair, laughing. Tim could see immediately that the man was smaller and more slender than him – a real surprise – but it did not prevent him from skidding to a halt. He didn't dare walk on the other's shadow for he knew who the man was. Tim recognised him from newspaper photographs. He knew he should keep apart from first-team players, so what happened next amazed him.

The small, slender, smiling man reached out and put his arm round Tim's shoulder.

"Hello, son. How are you then?" he asked.

"Fine, thank you, Mr Crooks."

"Good. What's your name then?"

"Ward."

"No, your first name."

"Tim."

"Are they looking after you, Tim?"

"Yes."

"Where's your digs then?"

"With Mrs Smith on Crewe Street."

"Oh, Mrs Smith," said Sammy Crooks, laughing loudly. "All the best players stay there."

"Did you?"

"Aye, man. She'll look after you. Good luck, son."

Sammy Crooks was quickly gone, but the spirit of a friendly man remained. Tim watched him go. "Perhaps I'll be able to see him play," he thought. That would be worth the dislocation, worth the initial feelings of loneliness, worth the estrangement from his family. Tim dwelled on what Sammy Crooks had said: Mrs Smith would look after him. Perhaps he could settle into this town. Maybe there was a chance after all.

Tim heard a knock on Mrs Smith's front door.

"I'll go," he said.

He opened the door casually, then stepped back in surprise. A Standard Twelve car was parked on the pavement, wedged between the lamp-post and Mrs Smith's front door with an inch to spare on either side. Tim was trapped in the house. Through the open passenger window, Tim heard the sound of laughter.

"Hello, there, Tim, son," said Sammy Crooks from the driver's seat. "Is young Alfie in?"

"I'll just get him."

Sammy Crooks and Alf Jeffries, both outside-rights from the north-cast, had a special relationship. They invited Tim to join them for a drink. Tim hesitated – it was a Friday night after all – but couldn't resist their company. Sammy moved the car, Tim and Alf got in.

"Right, where's it to be, lads? All-night cafe at Kilburn? A quiet country pub?"

Sammy knew all the people and all the places. He could take players backstage to meet the likes of Tommy Gamble or along to the golf club. Or he could take them for a quiet drink on a Friday night. Not that Sammy did anything quietly. He would buy a jug of beer and pass it round the pub. Generous to a fault.

He drove his car as if running down the wing with a ball – with short sharp sprints and plenty of swerving and weaving. He'd feint to go clockwise round an island and then go round the other way instead. The police recognised him, knew his number (DNU 995) and tolerated him. He was a god in Derby.

Tim's mind was on his "A" team game the next day. Alf was in the reserves. Sammy was playing for the first team.

"What about Arsenal tomorrow?" Tim asked Sammy.

"Oh, we'll piss over them," Sammy replied.

The next day Derby County beat Arsenal two-nil, and Tim understood that anything was possible.

3. Meeting Raich Carter

I wrote my first book at school during the 1955-56 football season and was embarrassed about it even then. Its 36 pages contained more than a hundred illustrations. I called the book *Football is My Life*, a title I must have borrowed from Len Hutton's autobiography, *Cricket is My Life*. My father kept a few autobiographies in the house, hidden among his many Book Club novels, and Len Hutton's was one of them.

The drawings in my book are either team pictures with all the players looking the same or, more likely, coloured action drawings. The team colours are remarkably accurate, but my captions sometimes fell short, especially when I tried to imitate the *Daily Express* method of putting a player's name in a white box next to his picture. For instance, my drawing of a goal by Johnny Hancocks for Wolves against Moscow Dynamo includes a Russian player called "Jackson". And when Brazil lost four-two at Wembley, my report credits their goals to Jackronia and Jassonte. (Belated apologies to Paulinho and Didi.)

I had a better grasp of the names of everyone at Leeds United because they came to see us on the first day of the 1955-56 season – Barnsley two, Leeds United one. My mother pointed out the distinguished Leeds United manager, a man with grey hair who wore a big camel coat and signed autographs left-handed.

"That's Raich," she said. "There he is."

It was obvious that Raich Carter was a family friend.

When I drew a Leeds United team picture in *Football is My Life*, I remembered names like John Charles, Jack Charlton and Albert Nightingale. In fact, eleven of the names on my picture are correct. The twelfth is Spatleduf.

I began to collect football programmes. Or my father collected them for me. I saved only Barnsley programmes at first, but we had a few from other clubs. One was from 18 August 1951 for the match between Hull City and Barnsley.

At inside-left for Hull City was Carter.

At right-half for Barnsley was Ward.

A girl called Jennifer Carter came to stay with us. She was a few years older than me.

I think I made a few connections.

At an early age I was also introduced to Raich Carter's *Soccer Star*, a magazine that rivalled Charles Buchan's *Football Monthly*. It added to my knowledge, and helped me answer my father's regular questions:

"Who's playing at Swansea on Saturday."

"How did St Johnstone get on?"

"Who has the best goal average in our division?"

"What's the bottom six look like in the First Division after today's results?"

My arithmetic improved. "Excellent, a very able worker," my teacher wrote on my report next to "mental and written arithmetic". She gave me 20 out of 20 for each subject.

Sometimes I asked my father questions.

"What's you best-ever team, Dad?"

"Of those I played with?"

"Yes."

He talked of Frank Swift and Joe Mercer and Peter Doherty and Tommy Lawton and Tommy Finney and Stanley Matthews. And he spoke a lot about Raich Carter.

Football, of course, is not "all about a ball". It's about the relationships that the ball provokes – player and team-mates, spectator and player, younger brother and older brother, manager and journalist, trainer and players, supporter and other supporters, father and son – and so, without knowing it, I began to admire Raich Carter, based on what had happened before I was born.

1937

The Baseball Ground was as hard as oak. Such was September. Tim, watching from the stand, marvelled at the way players controlled the bouncing ball as if speaking to it. There were so many internationals on the pitch that it took him ten minutes to work out who was who: Let's see, the tall fellow on our near wing is Dally Duncan of Scotland. And there's Sammy Crooks of England over the other side, and our other Scottish international, Charlie Napier. That must be Dai Astley of Wales in the middle. And there's Jack Barker and Eric Keen, of course, both English internationals.

And who've *they* got? Who's in the Sunderland team? Three internationals in the half-back line alone. He watched them for a minute or two, then looked upfield from the Sunderland half-backs and saw a player who made him gasp. Ah, that must be the chap they're all talking about, the one with the centre-parted brown hair and magnificent left foot. He's the young inside-forward who, in the last year or so, has played for a Championship team, captained the Cup-winners and played for England. He's the one who's done it all as a young man. He's Raich Carter.

And this is what Raich Carter's Cup-winning team looks like.

The two-two draw left Tim spellbound.

"I'll never be able to live with people like this," he thought, as the game progressed. "I'll never survive here."

But he watched closely all the same.
Just in case.

On the journey back from Blackburn Tim was quietly pleased with himself. He had played football in front of a large crowd and performed satisfactorily. Derby County Reserves had lost two-nil but it wasn't Tim who conceded the penalty and everyone said he had played well in his first game.

"You're here to stay now, son," someone said in the bath and Tim was delighted.

During that cool October evening he recalled that sentence many times, smugly reasoning that he was now a reserve-team player and "here to stay". He wondered what the manager's pal, the man who travelled with the reserves, would report back. He wondered what trainer Bill Bromage thought of it all. He wondered if he had impressed the other players. If everything was favourable, he would indeed be "here to stay".

Six weeks in the Colts team, playing against clubs like Basford United, Heanor Town and Chesterfield Ramblers, and now this. He was travelling long-distance with a group of men, playing in a team, keeping their company. It wasn't until he had said goodbye to them in Derby, walked to Crewe Street and retired to bed that he was on his own and able to think about what it meant. He undressed for the second time that day. This time, instead of changing into football kit, he put on pajamas, bought with the proceeds of his brief career as a professional footballer. He got into bed, his legs tired and fulfilled from the afternoon's running. He fully expected to have no mentality until morning, but something troubled him, niggled him, about those words: "You're here to stay now, son."

The warmth of these words turned to something more worrying. "Do I want to be in the Reserves to stay?" he asked himself. "Is that good enough?"

It was hard in this "huge" central industrial town. So much was different from Gloucestershire. On some days he heard a rumbling sound overhead and was mystified to find there were no aeroplanes in the sky. He didn't ask about the noise, but waited until others talked about it. "They must be testing engines at Rolls Royce today," he heard someone say, eventually. He learned about the best motor-car in the world, the best engines. He learned that Derby was not a centre for market-gardening or perfumery, although Royal Crown Derby produced beautiful pottery, but an industrial culture of "artificial silk" or "rayon" at British Celanese, lawn-mowers at Qualcast, malleable iron castings at Ley's, rolling-stock at the Midland Railway and heavy plant equipment at International Combustion. It was all new to him, except Ford & Weston, a building company which had sites at Derby *and* Cheltenham.

His strange rural accent was mimicked by the only other Gloucestershire boy on the staff and teased by some of the others. Alf Jeffries, who shared Tim's digs, had an acceptable north-east accent, and Scottish accents were also welcomed. So was Dai Astley's Welsh accent. But Tim's sing-song country voice sounded like he had a peppermint in his speech and the other players made him conscious of his speech. He said "wassps" stang people, they said "wosps". He was a country bumpkin because he hadn't known coalfields and grime, and no one could understood why the Devil's Chimney and elvers from the Severn Bore were important to him. In company, he was shy, but, on the football field, he could speak with a common accent. That was where he could belong, where he could show he deserved to stay.

Lying in bed, though, he knew he didn't want to stay in the reserve team. He wanted something else. An old fear of being taken away returned. He would have to play better, learn more, show them what he could do. He would have to be selected for the first team. That was the next step.

Having found his new goal, he drifted off to sleep with a sense of greater security.

"Bring out your dead," the voice yelled. "Bring out your dead."

The voice was accompanied by a deafening noise on Mrs Smith's door. The players inside had risen around 8.15 and had eaten a good breakfast of bacon and eggs. Now they laughed at the interruption.

"We're coming, Les," someone shouted back.

Tim and his fellow lodgers went to join Les Bailey at Mrs Smith's front door. Les Bailey was a burly man who played centre-half with enthusiasm and strength rather than subtlety. People said he lacked the class of Jack Barker, Derby County's first-choice international centre-half, but Bailey was a useful deputy. Tim was now accustomed to playing with big Les in the reserves. He could almost imagine Bailey beating on the opposition's door after the game – bring out your dead, bring out your dead – but there was nothing malicious about it.

The four men walked down Crewe Street. They called for goalkeeper Jack Kirby at the bottom of the street and Freddie Jessop round the corner. Tim had respect for Kirby. He still had sore memories from his first sprinting session at the club, when he had been teased into sprinting against "that lumbering goalkeeper" and the lumbering goalkeeper had beaten him by several pitch markings. Tim found out the hard way that Kirby was the fastest runner in the club.

Together, now six people going to work, they caught the bus to Melbourne Street. They were in good form. They had stories to tell about last night, and they knew other players would come to the ground with stories. "Joe" Johnson – called "Joe" because his brother Joe was a better-known player at Stoke – usually did impressions of what he'd seen.

They called for a few more colleagues: Jack Howe and Jackie Brinton at Mrs Nicholas's, Verdun Jones at Mrs Stubley's. They were close to a reserve team now, a successful reserve team, putting together a good string of results. They walked through the little streets and completed two sides of a square on the last part of their journey to work, receiving the comments of residents with good humour:

"Good morning."

"How are you this morning, then?"

"Are you on form this week?"

"I'll be watching you on Saturday."

When they reached the bakery they shouted to the girl friend of Teddy Roberts, who had recently been transferred to Coventry City.

"Hello, love."

"Good morning, lads," she replied.
"Is your bread stale yet?"
They arrived for work in good spirits, a bunch of working professionals, on the fringe of the first team.

1938

Early in the New Year, Tim was caught up in a low mood at the club. The Reserves were winning games but were still nearer the bottom of the Central League than the top. The first team were achieving only average success in the First Division and had been tumbled out of the FA Cup at home to Stoke City. The rest of the season looked dull.

On the Thursday afternoon after this FA Cup defeat, Tim faced his customary ordeal of visiting the home-team dressing-room in order to read team-sheets on the notice-board. Such was the demarcation between first and last teams that youngsters gave up billiard-cues when first-team players walked into the billiard-room. The first-team squad changed in the home-team dressing-room. The reserves, feeling like riff-raff, used the smaller away-team dressing-room.

Tim sneaked into the home-team dressing-room and looked down the list of players chosen for the Reserve team game against Aston Villa. His mood sank lower. There was no sign of his name. "I've been dropped," he thought. He looked on the "A" team list. Again no mention of his name. He skulked back out, his body feeling heavy. He returned to the away-team dressing-room and sat on the bench, trying to think what he might have done wrong. He was there for a minute, his own counsel, when he heard someone speak.

"Come on, son. Time for your massage."

Tim looked up. He saw Bill Bromage, the reserve-team trainer.

"Me?" Tim asked.

"Yes, son. Hurry along."

Tim stood up obediently. Only then did he understand the implications. There was a logical explanation for why his name was missing from the reserve and "A" team lists, and his mind made sense of the syllogism: he was being summoned for a massage; only first-team players had massages; therefore he was in the first team.

Rather than check his assumption immediately, he hurried along to the trainers' room and took his place in the queue. The hot, soapy, muscular fingers and thumbs of Dave Willis, the first-team trainer, worked for ten minutes on Tim's legs, back and front. Some of Tim's excitement was massaged away. At times he jumped. All the time, though, he wanted to read the notice-board. He needed to know if his assumption was correct.

The massage completed, Tim sneaked back into the home-team dressing-room and read the typed team-sheets more thoroughly. Yes, his name was there, listed sixth amongst the first teamers. Just above his name was "Bailey". Just below was "Crooks". Tim read the whole list – Wright, Bell, Howe, Nicholas, Bailey, Ward, Crooks, Hagan, Astley, Stockill and Duncan – and knew he could never forget the eleven names.

The nervousness started then. He was too overcome to notice that Derby

County's opponents were one of the most powerful teams in the country, the 1935-36 League Champions and current FA Cup holders. In two days time his most direct opponent would be an England international, a club captain who had achieved virtually everything football had to offer and was still only 24 years old. Had Tim realised all that, had he been pitched into battle on his own rather than as part of a team, he might have run for the hills around Charlton Kings and sought restoration of his courage. Instead he was swept along with Derby County routine, towards Saturday, the eternal focus of a footballer's week.

The next morning an élite steam train called the Cheltenham Flyer – capable of averaging 70 miles per hour on long journeys – sped into Cheltenham with a sign hanging above the nameplate.

Bill Andrews, senior, head shunter in Cheltenham, saw the two words on the sign – "Tim Ward" – and knew there was a message for him.

"What's it all about?" he asked.

"Haven't you heard?"

"No," said Bill.

"He's in the first team. Against Sunderland."

About the same time, that Friday, Tim was riding north with his colleagues. He was already friendly with some of the younger players, like Les Bailey and Jack Howe. He also knew and liked Jimmy Hagan, the north-east boy of frail physique who dribbled past players by the half-dozen and was busy developing a dry sense of humour ("Let's play this game at a fast pace and get it over with quickly").

The experienced professionals included Sammy Crooks, Dally Duncan and Jack Nicholas. The latter was a footballer of awesome tackle and kick. As his nickname of "Old Nick" suggested, he had a bit of devil in his play. Admirers of Nicholas called him rugged, robust, competitive and tough. Opponents saw him as crude, frightening and dirty. He had a kick that made pitches look small and a shoulder-charge that brought perimeter fences closer.

"You see that spire," said Sammy Crooks, as the train eased into Chesterfield and the crooked spire was visible. "One of Nick's penalties did that."

Tim looked at the hills behind Chesterfield railway station and began to relax. He knew he could never feel miserable in Sammy's company. Nothing seemed to bring Sammy Crooks down. Tim's boyhood hero felt that footballers were paid to entertain the public for an hour and a half each week, and they might as well continue the entertainment outside football-pitch hours. Sammy Crooks was a Stan Laurel figure with blue eyes and hair that stuck-up an inch and a half like a broom. It was impossible to part his hair. Sammy once walked into a barber's shop, sat down in the chair and said, "Gi' me one of them Sammy Crooks haircuts."

The train passed through towns with Third Division North teams, places like Doncaster and Rotherham. The experienced travellers pointed out where the football ground was, and perhaps a piece of trivia – "Brooky comes from Mexborough" – or they would tell a tale that came to mind. As the train approached the north-east, one or two players brought local knowledge to the scene. Jack Howe, Jimmy Hagan and Sammy Crooks were travelling towards home. So were manager

George Jobey and trainer Dave Willis. Tim, on the other hand, had never visited Britain's east coast and had never stayed in a hotel.

The team arrived at the Roker Hotel in Sunderland in the afternoon and Tim was booked into a room with Les Bailey. That evening George Jobey sensibly steered the players away from the negative-sounding play at the Roker Theatre – *We Who Are About To Die* with Preston Foster and Ann Dvorak – and took them across the River Wear to see Arthur Lucan and Kitty McShane in *Old Mother Hubbard*, the Christmas pantomime.

Late that Friday night, trainer Dave Willis shepherded his charges on to the correct tram-car – Dave knew the town well as he had played for Sunderland – and bought fifteen fares. The players sat upstairs and the tram-car was packed.

The conductor was counting the footballers when Sammy Crooks erupted into song at the top of his voice.

I wonder who's kissing her now,

"Oh, he's off," said one of the lads.

"Who does he think he is?" asked a local. "The Street-Singer?"

"More like the Street-Sweeper."

Sammy's words came over loud and clear, all over Sunderland. He had a very strong voice but completely without tune. Only confidence saw him through a song.

I wonder who's showing her how.

"He must be the worst singer ever capped by England."

"Worst in the Football League."

Sammy was on his feet now, waving his arms at the front of the upper deck. The other players and the Sunderland public joined in, blessedly drowning the sound of Sammy's voice. Everyone seemed to enjoy it, and, when the song was over, they talked about tomorrow's match.

"See you tomorrow," said one Sunderland supporter. "I hope you lose."

"You'll be like Rams to the slaughter."

"Hey, you can take a horse to water," replied Sammy Crooks. "But a pencil must be lead."

A few minutes before kick-off time (2.45), Tim, in accordance with his adopted superstition, pulled on shorts to complete his dressing for the match. When the bell went, the Derby lads wished him well, the manager wished him well, but no one said anything about what he should do when facing his direct opponent. No one told him how to handle an international player. No one said a word about Raich Carter.

They filed out. The sound of clattering studs echoed between the walls of the corridor, only it wasn't called a corridor: it was the "passage", and the "passage" separated private space from the public. Some men left the dressing-room as whimpering boys and then, a few yards later, met by a wall of noise, they became whole, maturing into grown-up egos, inflated like balloons.

Tim didn't notice the noise of the crowd at first. He noticed his nerves and he noticed the wind, a 60-mile-an-hour draught that bit into his knees. "There's always a wind at Roker," he remembered someone saying in the dressing-room. It was a good place for a wind museum.

Tim looked for ways to settle himself down. What he wanted was plenty of kicks in the kick-in, so he tried to be noticed by Harry Wright as the goalkeeper threw out the ball. They had only one ball to warm-up with. The captain carried it out.

Tim trotted around and did a few exercises. He looked at the eleven Sunderland players, the same eleven who had won the Cup at Wembley nine months before. Then, when he saw the Derby goalkeeper had the ball he put up his arms and called for a kick. Some players didn't want to touch the ball before kick-off. Tim was one who did.

Raich Carter won the toss for Sunderland and chose to play with the wind behind him. Tim's First Division professional career was soon under-way and he quickly realised that the wind was ironically working in his favour, for it wasn't easy for a star like Raich Carter to show his great skills with the ball swerving around and players making misjudgments. Early in the game, Johnny Mapson, the Sunderland goalkeeper, kicked the ball from his hands and it disappeared for a goal-kick at the other end. In contrast, Harry Wright of Derby County dawdled over his goal-kicks.

No one introduced Raich Carter to Tim Ward. They met after a minute or two of the game – "Carter beat Bailey but Ward was quickly in" – and yet another of football's many billion relationships began. Somehow Tim survived the first 45 minutes of his new job task. He defended countless corner-kicks and other Sunderland attacks. He battled against the wind, hounded players in red-and-white shirts and was complemented for one last-ditch sliding-tackle in his own goal area. Another time Harry Wright punched clear and the ball, held up by the wind, was sent back by Raich Carter. It bounced away off a goal-post. At half-time there was no score.

Early in the second half, Les Bailey challenged Sunderland centre-forward Bobby Gurney and the referee blew his whistle and pointed to the penalty spot. The Sunderland players looked surprisingly edgy. Bill Gorman set up the ball and walked back an eternal distance. He looked to be returning to his full-back position. Then he turned and ran towards the ball. Tim watched him run and run towards the stationary ball and attack it with all the power of a 1930s full-back and much of the direction. The ball sailed over the crossbar into the crowd.

Sunderland scored two goals in that second half, Derby County none. A two-nil Sunderland win was true to form. It took a good team to win at Roker Park. On the final whistle, Raich shook hands with Tim and walked away. He would remember the game for the penalty miss rather than his 20-year-old opponent. In general, though, it was the type of game that neutrals would forget.

Afterwards, Jack Howe invited Tim and Les Bailey to his family home at West Hartlepool, a short distance down the coast from Sunderland. They collected the return halves of their train tickets from manager George Jobey and arranged to return to Derby on the Monday.

That Saturday evening the three young working men sat with others in a working men's club in Hartlepool. Someone bought a round of drinks, and Tim allowed himself a Milk Stout. When it was on the table in front of him, he reflected on his weekend so far: a long enjoyable train excursion with the lads, checking into a posh hotel, an evening at the pantomime, a frolic on the tram-car ride home, a run-around with soccer's élite on Saturday afternoon and, now, an evening out in the pick of West Hartlepool's night spots. It was Saturday night at its best. As Tim raised his glass to his lips to savour the exquisite first frothy taste of his Milk Stout, he didn't believe that life could offer anything richer than a weekend like this. Whatever happened next, he had played First Division football in the same team as Sammy Crooks and on the same pitch as Raich Carter. No one could take that away. No one could erase the enjoyment of his weekend.

Tim was lucky. He had a second chance to play for the first team. A League game at Bolton Wanderers, abandoned earlier in the season, had been rearranged for the last Saturday of the month as both teams were out of the FA Cup. An outbreak of influenza – two first-team half-backs were ill – ensured that Tim stayed in the team at left-half, but the team was strengthened by the return of three internationals. One of them was inside-left Charlie Napier, a Scottish international known for his uncanny dribbling ability and nicknamed "Happy Feet" by supporters at Glasgow Celtic, his previous club.

On the journey to Lancashire, Tim learned the story of their first game at Bolton that season, a game abandoned after 37 minutes. Bolton were leading by two goals – and should have been further ahead – when fog came down and the referee suggested the teams went off. George Jobey sprinted into the dressing-room to give the players a rare team-talk: "Get in the bath. Don't worry about getting out of your boots. Straight in the bath." A few minutes later, when the referee came to call them back to the field, the Derby County lads were singing in the bath and the game had to be abandoned.

Derby County played the re-arranged match in black-and-white striped shirts to avoid a colour clash. They kept their usual black shorts, which still clashed with Bolton's dark navy. After 89 minutes of the game, Derby County led two-nil through two goals by Welsh international centre-forward Dai Astley. Play was on the Derby right wing, Astley was chasing his hat-trick, and Tim, concentrating on the play, was surprised when two arms came from behind him and grabbed his chest in an enormous bear hug. A Scottish accent whispered in his ear: "What do you think then, Tim? It's your first win bonus."

He recognised the voice.

"We're still playing," Tim said.

Charlie Napier simply laughed and let go.

Edinburgh's Waverley station overflowed with people. Tim couldn't believe it. Late on a Saturday night and such a reception. The whole city had turned out. Nothing but cheering crowds of people.

"We're popular up here," said one Derby player.

"We must be," Tim thought, but he couldn't understand it. Earlier that day Derby County had lost four-one at Preston North End, and a weakened Preston North End at that, as four Preston players were away playing for Scotland at Wembley. Tim was a bit despondent afterwards. He was glad he had been retained on a new contract for the next 12 months, pleased that Derby County issued their retained list earlier than most clubs. Otherwise he might have been worried. After 14 successive League appearances, he was being left out for this friendly at Hearts.

A crescendo of noise reached Tim's train. The crowds approached. Hundreds of glengarries flew up into the air to find new owners when they came down. Tim had no inkling that his first visit to Scotland, his first visit to another country, could be like this.

"This is all for us, is it?" Tim asked.

"I doubt it," someone replied. "Tommy Walker's further down the train."

Tommy Walker had scored the only goal of the Scotland-England international earlier that day. And Tommy Walker was a Scot.

1944

Almost exactly six years after his first contacts with international inside-forwards – Raich Carter, Charlie Napier, Tommy Walker – Tim witnessed a piece of inside-forward play that he would remember for ever.

Derby County's guest inside-left stood with his back to Tim, eyes on the ball at his feet. The Sheffield Wednesday right-half had his eyes on the same ball, and planned to stop the ball coming into the penalty area. He looked confident that he could do it. Sheffield Wednesday were losing this wartime game two-one but could still come back.

The Derby man shimmied his hips and shoulders. His white shirt rustled. He was going to his right and the Wednesday player's body was lured that way. The defender's left foot twitched, ready to pounce because he thought he had the Derby player covered, but the ball was gone. The man in the white shirt had already created the narrowest of gaps, a slight sight of the goal, and it was enough. From twenty yards the ball was in the net. Even Tim, watching closely, was unsure how it had happened.

The defender looked amazed.

"I bet you couldn't do that again in a million years," he said to his opponent.

It was the sort of challenge that suited Raich Carter's confidence. Two minutes later he was back in the same spot, shimmying, feinting, until he saw that same brief glimpse of the goal. He jinked as though going to his right, then flicked the ball back with his left foot and hit it all in one movement. Another twenty-yard shot. Another goal. Four-one.

"Do you want to see it a third time?" Raich asked the Sheffield Wednesday player.

Tim, a few yards away, laughed to himself.

Raich was on his side now. If only as a guest player.

1945

Tim arrived home three ration-ridden shopping days before Christmas. He studied the Derby County fixture-list. His club had five games in 14 days and he would play in them all. He had two new Derby County colleagues now, both signed recently, two inside-forwards with no betters, and the manager wanted a wing-half like Tim to give them the ball.

Both Peter Doherty and Raich Carter had played for Derby County as guests while working at Loughborough. Raich Carter's hair was grey now. During the war he'd fought fires, lost a house in a bombing raid, become a father, joined the RAF and had been transferred from Sunderland to Derby County. Tim's first game back was Raich's first game as a signed Derby County player, but Raich had had very little sleep, and looked very tired.

Birmingham one, Derby County nil.

Derby County were playing to 30,000 crowds now. On Christmas Eve, they stayed at a posh London hotel, ready for the next day's match with Tottenham Hotspur. The Middlesbrough team were staying at the same hotel. One of their players came in at 10am to eat breakfast. A bleary-eyed trainer, up all night waiting, confronted him.

"I've been to mass," said the player.

On Christmas Day, in the dressing-room at White Hart Lane, Tim watched Peter Doherty as he changed, which was always at the last moment. Peter arrived in a dressing-room only 15 minutes before kick-off, having finally said goodbye to his many friends outside. He could change quickly. He didn't need time to bandage his knees like Leon Leuty did. At Tottenham, however, trainer Dave Willis thought Peter had a problem.

"Have you seen your boots?" Willis asked.

"What's the matter with them?"

"You're missing three studs on one and two on the other."

Peter held the boots as though he was a faith-healer taking the hands of a blind man. "Dave," he said. "If you can play, you can play."

That day Peter Doherty scored once, and Derby County won five-two. Tim knew that a player of Peter's class could adapt to all conditions and footwear. His balance was so good that he could play in carpet-slippers on snow. Or so Tim believed.

They beat Tottenham Hotspur at home on Boxing Day. Another lock-out. Another ferocious left-footed goal from Raich Carter. War-workers, women, soldiers on leave and the recently demobbed converged on the Baseball Ground. Carter and Doherty convinced all Derby County fans that a wonderful year was waiting. It was numbered 1946. Hope had been gained by the war effort and the success of Rolls-Royce engines. The new year in Derby promised Carter and Doherty and Attlee and peace.

Brentford were beaten next, three-two on the 29th day of December. One of the Brentford players made the mistake of telling Raich Carter and Peter Doherty that they were "too old" and "past it". Peter Doherty scored a goal, Raich scored two memorable ones and Derby were three-nil up before half-time. Three successive wins with the same team. They were ready for Derby County's first FA Cup game for seven years. Tim was as ready as any of them.

1946

It was perfect. It was easy. It was what Tim had looked forward to since he was a boy. The best two inside-forwards in the world (he thought) and, on the right wing, back after injury, his boyhood hero Sammy Crooks. The third round of the FA Cup and a runaway win. So simple, so simple. You watch the play, get the ball and give it to brilliant players. You never waste a pass. Your team-mates work like geniuses. What a wonderful facile game. The sheer beauty of belonging. The pleasure of being part of a team.

So Tim won the ball or took a pass from a team-mate, and knew, just knew, that Carter and Doherty were waiting for that same ball. At times he felt he should be paying to see them. At close quarters he was impressed with their sense of balance. Both could appear committed to moving one way, then switch without falling over. Raich Carter had no great pace, but he always seemed completely isolated when he received the ball. He created the space for himself, as though he were watching the film for the tenth time and already knew the scenes. In his own half he used the ball, effectively and efficiently. No messing about. No mannerisms. When he received the ball, he knew who was unmarked, who was in the best position and where the ball was going. He could pass the ball long distances, left-footed, across the field to the left wing or perfectly weighted to the right, into the stride of Sammy Crooks. Or he could push it short, to Peter or centre-forward Jack Stamps. Near the Luton penalty area, however, Raich was less conscious of where his team-mates were running, more conscious of where the goal-posts were staying. He used tricks only to create shooting chances, swerving deceptively, dummying, making room for his powerful left-foot shot. He wanted a position to shoot rather than to make a pass. He knew that shooting was yet another strength in his game, and, more than anything, he wanted to win.

Peter Doherty was his complement. Peter had tricks for wherever he went, and that was all over the field, his stamina without precedent, his enthusiasm infectious. He drew back his foot as if to kick the ball, then kicked six inches behind the ball and took it gently on instead. The same trick with either foot. He leaned over the ball, protected it, made sure opponents kept their distance. And when he scored a goal it was more likely to be from five or six yards, having taken the ball past a few players before flicking it past the goalkeeper (if the goalkeeper was still on his feet).

Most teams had one inside-forward who did more "fetching and carrying" and another further upfield as a foil to the centre-forward. This team had two inside-forwards who did everything. This team could run away with a game, as they did that day at Luton.

Luton Town nil, Derby County one.

Luton Town nil, Derby County two.

Luton Town nil, Derby County three.

Luton Town nil, Derby County four.

Luton Town nil, Derby County five.

Luton Town nil, Derby County six.

Carter and Doherty scored that day, and Jack Stamps scored four. It was only the first leg of the third round FA Cup tie – 1946 ties were home and away for economic reasons – but no one believed that Luton could go to the Baseball Ground and win by six goals.

"Who do you fancy for the Cup, Sammy?" someone asked.

"I honestly don't know," Sammy Crooks replied, "who will be runners-up to us."

The answer was Charlton Athletic.

4.
More Than Picking The Team

I remember an incident when I was very young. I might have been four, I might have been more, but I know my father's office at Oakwell Stadium, Barnsley, seemed huge to me that day. He shared it with the club secretary and the receptionist, but they weren't there, and he left me alone while he went to see the directors in the board room next door.

"I won't be long," he said.

When I heard distressed voices next door, I began to cry. The office had nothing to interest me. I couldn't stop crying. The more I looked around the office, the less it offered me. The voices next-door continued, too grown-up, too muffled for me to understand.

What was going on next door?

I soaked my handkerchief and didn't know where to cry next. I couldn't go into the board room. I waited and waited. Hours went by, or was it minutes? When my father returned I was drained of tears.

"Sorry I took so long," he said. "One of the directors took poorly. I had to help him."

Another time, we were in the office and the club secretary came in.

"Have you sold them all, Raymond?" someone asked him.

"All except one. I can't find anybody else. And it's only one ticket per person."

"I'll have the last one for my lad," my father said.

He bought me a ticket in the club's Grand National sweep.

A horse called Mr What.

The horse won.

Later, I wondered what the players made of it.

In my copy of *The First English Workbook* I completed one of the exercises.

My name is Andrew Ward.
I am seven years old.
I go to Wilthorpe School.
My hair is dark.
My eyes are brown.
I have no brothers or sisters.
I get up at eight o'clock.

I go to bed at eight o'clock.

Another exercise asked for Yes/No answers.

Little girls help their mothers?

"Yes," I answered.

Boys play at aeroplanes?

"Yes."

Dogs say goodbye?

"No."

Fathers go to work?

"Yes."

The teacher went round the class asking us what work our fathers did.

"Coal-miner," said a boy in my row.

"Miner," said the girl in front of me.

"Football manager," I said.

I thought it was a normal occupation, but necks swivelled and eyes were upon me.

"What does your father do then?"

"He picks the team."

"Is that all?"

"I suppose."

I knew, of course, that he watched Barnsley and other teams play football. I knew he signed players. I imagined he spent the rest of his time sitting at his desk with a piece of paper in front of him, writing out combinations of players that went together to form "his team".

"What's your team for Saturday," I asked him, several times each week.

"Toogood, Nogood and Getgood," he would start. "Freeman, Hardy and Wills. Greenhouse, Glasshouse, Doghouse, Sweetshop and Doorknob."

"I don't believe you."

"We're trying to sign a Russian centre-forward called Bangitinski."

He told me his team when he was ready, just early enough to give me a start on my class-mates. It was a privilege second to none, or so I thought at the time.

My parents valued "good manners". When I grew tall enough to reach the table with my elbows, they worked hard on me at meal-times.

"Elbows off the table," they told me, without raising a voice.

I put my elbows on the table a lot. They told me a lot.

A football manager came for lunch. The prospect of spending almost £30,000 of his club's money was on his mind. After the meal, he sat back, lit a cigar and then leaned forward to collect his thoughts on the player in question.

"Elbows off the table," I yelled at him.

He jumped back like he'd been hit on the back with a medicine-ball.

As I grew older, I was able to see my father at work. I didn't see him pick the team but I saw him answer letters and make telephone calls in his office.

"My name is Ward," he would say, when connected. "Barnsley Football Club."

Lily Johnson, the secretary-receptionist, showed me how to make a stencil and run off a few hundred copies from it. A pile of youth-team programmes grew in front of me.

One time I went with my father to a supporters' club gathering. He talked to a dozen people about the five-a-side method of training. Then he answered questions. I remember him saying "touch wood" on three occasions and reaching for the back of the chair. I don't remember much else he said, though I think there was something about the Hungarians beating the English at Wembley. Otherwise, the nearest I got to talking tactics with him was at meal-times, when he set up a half-back-line of salt, pepper and vinegar. He said they played for Cruet Alexandra.

I watched him train with young players one fine Tuesday evening. He talked a lot about his young players. The words "youth policy" were part of my upbringing. Every time a Barnsley player received an England Youth cap I sensed the thrill it gave him. We began to talk about the Busby Babes and the Cullis Cubs. Ah, I concluded, the more young players in a team, the better the manager.

On Saturdays of home games my mother served my father with an early lunch and he left in good time. We followed later. Our bus-stop was thirty yards away. The buses were generally full. Sometimes someone stopped to give us a lift.

At the football ground, I had a seat alongside my mother, at the back of Centre Stand. She wanted to stretch her rug over my bare knees, but I did my utmost to resist because the players on the pitch didn't cover up their knees. I stood up some of the time, but wasn't tall enough to worry the people behind. The pitch seemed a hundred miles away, but I swear I saw every expression on every player's face. I recognised our players by their shape and movements. I gripped a programme tightly in my fingers, bent back at the middle pages, and after 20 minutes I knew our opponents man for man. At my side, my mother was generally quiet, occasionally digging me with an elbow when saying "Go on, boy," in an excited voice.

One time my father collected me from home and drove me to a home game as my mother couldn't go.

After he had parked the car, I realised my season-ticket was at home.

"Just tell the man on the stairs who you are," said my father in an unusually impatient voice. Kick-off was less than half an hour away.

I wanted him to come with me. I didn't know what to say to the steward on the Main Stand stairs, especially when I saw a few people around him. Instead I ran up the stairs.

"Stop that boy," someone shouted.

"Manager's son," I replied from the top of the steps, making a bigger spectacle of myself.

Someone recognised me. I was allowed to continue.

As I grew up, and began to understand more of football, I loved sitting next to him on scouting trips. His relaxation was watching other managers' teams, and his sporadic comments floated my way. Sometimes he was critical of players – "don't give it him, son, he's unmarked" – and sometimes critical of spectators. If a spectator said, "That was nearly a good ball," my father would ridicule him out of the corner of his mouth: "You can't have nearly a good ball. Either it is or it isn't."

When watching local games he would cringe when a trainer came on the field and tried to push a player's head between his legs.

"That's the worst thing you could do," he said.

We watched Chesterfield play Wrexham. A Wrexham forward chased a long pass down the centre. The Chesterfield goalkeeper slipped as he came out. The ball ran past the goalkeeper and would have gone into the net on its own but the Wrexham forward tried to make sure. He put his foot on the ball and fell flat on his face. The ball squirmed out behind him towards the Chesterfield goalkeeper.

"We'll have him next season," a Chesterfield supporter shouted.

My father giggled for 20 minutes and explained how Chesterfield free-transferred five forwards each season and signed five more.

On such trips I learned a lot about each club's tea-room provisions, like Shentall's pork-pie at Chesterfield and custard-tarts at Rotherham. In tea-rooms and boardrooms my father was relaxed when trading tales with other managers. People came up to us and mumbled inside stories about undercounter payments and other inducements.

"So he went off to sign this England Youth lad and he knew there were a lot of other clubs after him. He got near where he lived but he didn't know the address, so he stopped and asked someone the way. 'You'll recognise the street,' this chap said. 'It's the one with all his new cars down it.'"

We travelled a lot by car. Always there were football analogies. If we saw roadside notices at pubs saying, "No coaches," he would reassure us that it was alright because he was a manager. If we saw a hare run across the road, he'd say, "Pass my football boots, I'll run and catch it."

Sometimes, on family outings, my father's acute hearing would register periodic blasts of a referee's whistle, a soft thud of boot on ball and players' shouts. He would make a detour to find a distant game. The games were usually no more than local games, the pleasure coming from my father's ability to predict players' actions: "Watch this teacake on the right wing. Here he comes. Watch him trip over the ball."

My mother and I would laugh as players made comical errors on cue.

I dreamed of my father finding a star player in a local game. But he never did. Only "teacakes".

Occasionally, though, he would come home and say those magic words: We've signed a player.

"A first-team player?"

"Yep."

"What position?"

"Guess."

My programme collection blossomed. I began to realise that I could collect at least one of every Football League club. I had an elusive dozen or so, and my father suggested I write to clubs enclosing a stamped-addressed envelope. I did this, and was ecstatic when mail began arriving at our house. I'd never received mail before.

My new programmes were for matches between teams unfamiliar to me. They looked so foreign that I stared increduously at every cranny. I loved each one dearly. I cherished my Crewe Alexandra versus Hartlepools United programme. It stretched to 12 pages and I hungrily devoured the words that were scattered between the 31 advertisements.

"Dad, did you know that 1,558 people saw Crewe's North Regional League game against York City Reserves."

The section called "Club Notes and Comments" made compulsive reading: "Our visitors tonight, Hartlepools United, are having a very thin time. We welcome them to Gresty Road and wish them better luck after tonight's game."

I was fascinated by an advertisement in the Swansea Town programme that was upside-down. A year later my father came back with another Swansea Town programme. The same advert was still upside-down. Only then did I realise that it was no accident.

My father brought me other souvenirs. When he went to Sheffield Wednesday for the opening of the new stand – "not a pillar in sight" – he came back with a souvenir brochure. The brochure gave historical highlights, like Wednesday's first football match: "Played against Dronfield at Dronfield on 31st December 1867. Wednesday won by 1 goal to four 'rouges'."

"Dad, what's a rouge?"

I was beginning to realise that football managers didn't know everything.

With hindsight, I recognise that many tasks of my father's job were no different from those carried out by other company managers: promoting a good company image to the public and the press; assembling a successful product and increasing the number of paying customers; recruiting and transferring staff; solving staff problems; keeping an eye on the competition; dealing with correspondence and administration; and watching the budget. Not all company managers are so obsessed with Saturdays, however, and few are judged not only by profit but also by clear measures of success such as points, League position and progress in the FA Cup. As a child, these measures of success were virtually all I understood, despite being so exposed to opportunities to observe the rest. Eventually I grasped the complexities. My father must have been the same. There must have been a point where he realised that a manager's job was more than picking the team.

1935

"We haven't seen you down here the last fortnight," said George Carr, the Cheltenham Town manager. "Where've you been?"

"I've been playing football," Tim replied, nervously. He hadn't expected to be missed.

"You've not been training."

"Er, no. Well, I couldn't get a game. I couldn't see the sense."

"Oh, come down training. We'll look after you."

The manager paused. Then, with an autocratic air patented by football managers, he added a comment: "You're a wing-half, you know."

"Am I?"

"Aye."

They reached the dressing-rooms and the conversation was over. Tim was left to hang on the words.

Later that evening, George Carr drove his car to the edge of the Whaddon Road pitch and nestled it between the scaffolding poles (supposedly there to keep the crowd off the pitch). The car's headlights, shining across the pitch, were enough to allow a few minutes' ball practice for half a dozen players. Accustomed to playing under street lighting on a far worse surface, used to kicking substitute footballs, these players were perfectly happy playing a headlight friendly. Tim didn't complain. To him it was a treat.

The next Saturday brought a bigger treat. He was selected as first-team reserve and given ten shillings, almost as much as he was earning at Lindner's box factory. The occasion was marred by a minor accident. He burned his bag on the gas fire in the dressing-room and used most of his energy concealing the faux pas from the first-team players. Some of his ten shillings went on a new bag for his kit. He also made a vow. He would never miss a Tuesday or Thursday training session again.

He was walking along Prestbury Road when he heard a shout.

"Hey, Tim, wait for me."

Tim looked round, and saw a distant, shadowy figure further down the road. He couldn't tell who it was. As the man came closer, Tim recognised George Carr.

"Evening, son," the manager said. "I saw it was you."

Tim was baffled. "How could you see it was me?" he asked. "It's dark."

"I'd know that walk anywhere."

Tim felt self-conscious. Then he thought about the older man. George Carr looked more like a professional jockey, small, with the awkward, rolling walk of a sailor. They said he'd broken a leg twice at Middlesbrough. Or was it three times?

"Listen to who's talking," said Tim.

They fell into walking harmony, a bow-legged crippled manager and a pin-toed hopeful youth.

1937

Tim knew he was risking the sack from his job. He had already attended one trial, at Leicester, and taking a day off proved a reckless move in an era of unemployment and no official holidays. His foreman was unrelenting: one more time and it was the sack.

So here it was.

He had been disappointed not to hear anything from Leicester City. He was happy enough with his performance that day, and was congratulated by other players when he sat in the bath after the game. He liked to think that the clubs could not agree terms. Of course, it might have been that he was not good enough.

He was more confident now, no longer overawed by top-class grounds or international-class players. Hadn't Ipswich brought three former internationals to Whaddon Road? And Chelsea had had two in their reserve team for a February friendly. It had been a good season for Tim, though he hadn't grown any heavier or more muscular. He was still slightly built and wiry. The only change in his physique was in the shape of his nose. It had been broken twice.

A day off work was worth the risk. George Carr knew the scout well. Jackie Whitehouse was his name. Derby County of all clubs. Tim wasn't going to miss this game at Birmingham. Wearing his old suit, he travelled silently through the Gloucestershire and Worcestershire countryside.

In the dressing-room he pretended to be professional. He dressed in the white shirt, black and white socks, boots and shinpads, and then, copying a respected colleague, he put on his shorts last. He was ready. With ten strangers he went out to face Moor Green in the Midlands Midweek League.

A new player's first kick can be an object of scrutiny – by colleagues, spectators and officials. In his first game for Derby County "A" team, Tim Ward introduced himself to the ball at the edge of the Moor Green penalty area. He ran to it and kicked it sweetly. As the ball sailed towards the goal-net, Tim watched its course fondly. A goal with his first kick. Not a peculiar goal, like the ones he was used to scoring, but one to be proud of. Doing his utmost to conceal a grin, he turned expressionless and ran back towards the halfway-line, feigning the appearance of a man who scores a goal with his first kick every week.

Derby County "A" won the game five-two. Afterwards, Tim and his new colleagues were taken to the Grand Hotel, Birmingham. Tim had never been to a hotel before. He approached the meal timidly, staring cautiously at unusual features like white tablecloths and toothpicks.

When the meal was finished, he was taken into another room, where he met a small but imposing man with charisma and presence. The stranger had a large oval face and a strong neck, and behaved with ultimate authority. This was George Jobey, manager of Derby County. Tim also met a Cheltenham Town official and joined up with Jackie Whitehouse, who he had first met after a game at Cheltenham. It was Whitehouse, along with the commanding figure of Jobey, who, in an ante-room of the Grand Hotel in Birmingham, showed Tim where to sign a contract as a full-time professional footballer. Tim signed his name. He did not read a word of the printed form.

George Jobey laid down two white five-pound notes.

"What are these for?" Tim asked.

"They're yours," said Jobey. "It's your signing-on fee."

Tim stared at the notes increduously. It was the strangest thing yet that he had seen in this hotel. Ten pounds was too good to be true. There had to be a catch. No one in Cheltenham would believe him. A windfall of this size would seem like stolen money.

"We'll have some nice digs for you when you come through on Monday," George Jobey said. He spoke in a north-east accent but Tim was too inexperienced to notice.

There were three weeks of the season left. Tim did not realise that he was signing a contract for only three weeks.

The next day he faced his foreman at Lindner's.

"You're sacked," the foreman said.

"No, I'm not," Tim replied, with uncharacteristic assertiveness.

"Yes, you are."

"No, I'm not, because I'm leaving anyway." He grew taller in that moment and thrust out his chest. "I'm going to be a professional footballer with Derby County."

Equipped with golf clubs borrowed from one of the other footballers, it was his first time on a golf course. On the first tee of Markeaton Golf Club, he put the ball on the ground and stood alongside it, side-on to the fairway. Facing him, next to the tee, was a maintenance hut. Alongside the hut stood manager George Jobey and trainer Dave Willis.

"You'll need a tee for the ball," one of the other players advised.

"Oh."

The golf-tee went in the ground, and he was ready again. He addressed the ball and took a good swing with the borrowed club. He shanked his shot and the ball flew off at a sharp angle to the right. It bounced off the maintenance-hut, hit a nearby fence and cannoned across to the other side of the tee. George Jobey and Dave Willis lowered their hands from their faces and looked across with some surprise.

"I hope he's a better footballer," Jobey said.

In the gymnasium, throwing a medicine-ball to another player, Tim was whistling, pleased with the way he had been playing for the Derby County Colts.

"Just a minute," shouted an officious voice at the door. "What's all the noise about?"

The players looked up. They saw George Jobey, the manager. They stood to attention.

"If we want a bloody band down here I'll get it organised," said Jobey. "You come here to train." The manager looked at Tim and pointed menacingly with his forefinger. "I'll see you in my office."

"Oh, no," Tim thought. "What have I done wrong? Was it the whistling? No, it must be more than that. Has he noticed the ankle injury I've been trying to hide? Am I not coming back next year after all?"

The area under the Baseball Ground grandstand was roughly divided into two halves: the dirty half contained dressing-rooms, trainer's room, boot-room, laundry-room and gymnasium; the clean half contained the offices, the paper work, the directors' rooms (although the club secretary was oddly located in the half with the dressing-rooms). Tim walked fearfully along the corridor, across the divide, to George Jobey's office. He suspected that the best policy was to avoid the manager as much as possible. It reminded him of school, or the threat of boxing-gloves at home.

"How long have you been here now?" George Jobey asked Tim.

"Er, about a month, Sir."

"Well, it's about time you went home to see your people. Ask the secretary for your train fare and go home this weekend."

"Yes, sir."

"Oh, and one more thing." He ran his eyes up and down Tim's slight frame. "Get some Milk Stout down you. Some Fountain's Milk Stout. Build yourself up. I'll have word with the trainer and see what we can do for you."

"Yes, Sir."

Tim had never touched a drop of alcohol in his life. Now he felt obliged to drink Milk Stout. It could have been worse. Jobey's early advice to another player was to have his bad teeth taken out and send the bill to the club. The dentist took them all out.

The trainer encouraged Tim to eat sugar and glucose for energy, steaks to build him up, and capsules of cod-liver oil and malt. The assistant trainer took him on to the terraces and taught him breathing exercises to help him put on weight. They all wanted him to put on weight. Tim started checking his body daily for signs of change, hoping to divert the trainer's attention. He was reassured when he noticed that another slightly-built youngster, Jimmy Hagan, was the guinea-pig for all the latest weight-inducing diets and looked to have little chance of making the grade without another stone or two.

Tim had felt like sneaking home during those first few weeks – he certainly missed the Andrews family – and George Jobey's timely offer was exactly what he needed. He slipped back to Cheltenham, reminded himself that he still had his £10 signing-on fee in his new account at the Cheltenham & Gloucester Building Society, and recognised again his yen to play football.

He was lonely that summer, playing cricket and walking the fields. For the first time in his life he lacked the imposed structure of school or work. At the start of the summer he even wished he was back at Lindner's; by the end he was looking forward to playing football again. He thought that everyone at Derby County shared his ambitions of winning the League Championship and the FA Cup.

A strange ground, a first visit, a new experience. He saw the door open for trainer Bill Bromage, revealing the hubbub inside, a smoky haze and well-dressed people.

"Now then, trainer," Tim heard someone say from within the room. "What would you like to drink?"

"I'd like a Sandeman's port," Bromage replied.

The door shut as Tim walked by. For all he knew, Sandeman's port was an east-coast harbour. The episode puzzled him, especially his brief sight of what lay behind a door marked "Board Room".

1938

A director walked into the dressing-room.

"I've backed a horse for you this afternoon," he said.

"What is it?" asked one of the players.

"I won't tell you now. I'll tell you afterwards."

The experienced players knew not to ask more. The horse would probably win… if they did.

George Jobey went straight to the point. He came after Tim with his index finger pointing at the youngster's chest, even though it was the last home game of the season and Derby County had little to play for. They were halfway up the League and halfway down.

"I know where you were the other night," he said. "Thursday night. You can cut that out."

Tim immediately felt guilty that he and Les Bailey had sneaked into the Black Swan on Siddals Road for a Thursday evening drink. The pub, nicknamed the "Dirty Duck", was run by Les Bailey's girlfriend's parents. Tim was happy to tag along but knew now that it was difficult to have a quiet drink without being recognised. There was nowhere to hide. George Jobey obviously had informants everywhere. Tim thought it was just Friday nights that he was being watched. He had heard that Jobey sent a one-eyed man to check on the players on Fridays. More than one player had been spotted coming home in the early hours. "If you say anything, I'll knock out your other eye," one stop-out said.

Being in a pub was as visible as being on a football pitch, and Tim was embarrassed by it all. One week, when his photograph was in the local newspaper three times, he was so shy that he didn't want to walk down the street.

When they played at Grimsby, they ate lunch at a hotel in Lincoln, or should have done. When George Jobey returned from drinking his quota, the players were still waiting to be served. An hour had passed.

"*What*? You haven't had lunch?" erupted Jobey. His ubiquitous finger summoned a waiter. "Fetch the manager," Jobey ordered.

The waiter returned with the head waiter.

"Are you the manager?" Jobey asked.

"No, Sir, I'm the head waiter,"

"*I told him to fetch the manager*," yelled Jobey, finger pounding the table. "And when I say *the manager*, I mean *the manager*."

The manager came. Only one voice was heard: "And you've got five minutes to feed them or I'll make sure no football club comes here ever again. We'll be back at seven tomorrow, *and God help you* if there's not a meal ready for us."

Tim mused over his manager's outburst. "I hope I don't play a bad game tomorrow," he thought.

1939

The Good Friday game at Portsmouth finished at 4.40pm. The fixture-list forced them to travel back to Derby quickly, arrive about 11pm, sleep at the Midland Hotel, set off for Liverpool at 9am, play another away game and return the same day.

They tried to relax on the journey back to Derby. George Jobey said the club would stand the players a round of drinks. Then the manager stretched out across the seats. When the waiter brought in a second round of drinks, Jobey opened his eyes and spoke: “Are you having another drink, lads? Remember you pay for this one out of your own pockets.”

Jobey went back to sleep.

Sometimes, when travelling by train after an away game, Tim wondered if they would have a meal. Then, at the next stop, on came individual baskets of food, each one containing steak, chips and all the trimmings. Empty baskets were deposited at the next station.

At times like that he realised someone was looking after him.

5.

Innocence Nil, Realism One

In my seventh year I started watching Barnsley home games regularly. It was 1955-56, and we were in the Second Division. I assumed we always won. Then we played Bury.

We led three-one at half-time and Bury missed a penalty early in the second half. Probably their last chance, a few supporters said. But it wasn't. They scored twice late in the game, and scrambled a three-three draw.

I stood up after the game, tried to be a man, tried not to cry.

"Don't worry, young un," said a loyal supporter known to everyone as Uncle Chuck. "They'll do better next week."

"It's alright," said my mother. "It's only a game."

I wanted to believe them.

I don't think I missed a home game that season. I began to notice opponents as well as my Barnsley heroes. My homework was to spot their goalscorers as well as ours, a task no doubt motivated by my father's discussion of opponents when he summarised games in our living-room.

When West Ham scored a goal at Oakwell, I kept my eyes on the goalscorer until I could see his number. I looked up his name in the programme, remembered it. Albert Foan didn't score many goals for West Ham, but that one at Barnsley was important to me.

After the game, some family friends gave my mother and I a lift home in a car. I wanted to check my information, so I asked them who had scored for West Ham. No one knew.

Later I asked my father.

He knew of course.

And, yes, I had it right.

If I wanted to be a football manager, like my father, I had to remember every kick of every game.

Occasionally my father stayed out overnight. It was called "a long-distance away game". When he returned I was allowed to search the pockets of his overcoat for a memento of the trip, like a ticket or the match programme.

I constructed images of places he visited – Fulham, Middlesbrough, Bristol, West Ham, Plymouth, Swansea. My conceptions were based on how long my father was away, the treasure trove he brought back, the result and his mood on return. The friendliness of the other manager helped. Sometimes they had traded jokes.

"Did you hear there's a football manager in hospital?" he said, when he came back from Swansea.

"No."

"Yes, he's got a bad side."

Scotland was a place of funny-sounding names. My father, back from a scouting trip, would talk of Auchenshuggle, Clachnacuddin and Ecclefechan. When we looked at Scottish League results he would tickle me with his pronunciations: Stenhousemanure, Patrick Thistle and Cowdenbeneath.

I decided to support St Johnstone. Maybe it was because Manchester City's Bobby Johnstone had scored in two successful FA Cup Finals, so the name had a ring of success to it. Maybe, like my Australian choice, Box Hill, it was because I could spell the name.

"I know how we can get you home," my father said. "We can take you on the bus."

I was trapped at the football ground. A few unscheduled telephone calls, a crisis or two, and my father had no time to drive me home before the team left for an away game.

The team coach was waiting. It would pass our house.

I got on the bus and sat near the front. The players looked enormous. I wondered if my presence was affecting them.

I doodled with my crayons and stared out of the window. I could feel the tension. The noise of the radio came from the back of the bus.

"... United include 18-year-old..."

The bus stopped specifically for me. I got off and professional footballers stared at me through the bus windows. For a moment our roles were reversed. My father got off too, saw me safely across the road, then went back to the players.

Against my mother's wishes, I kicked a balloon around the house. A balloon couldn't damage anything, could it?

As I kicked the balloon, I kept my eyes on it, just like coaches said you should, pirouetted on one foot and met the balloon perfectly with the other, two or three feet from the ground, for a sweetly struck volley.

Ccrrraaaassssshhhhhh!

There had been six glasses and a decanter on that low table. My father had brought them back from a tour of Czechoslovakia just after the war. Not a glass survived my game. I think that's when my mother started collecting brass and pewter instead of glass.

"Not in the house, Andrew," she said, repeatedly, whenever she saw me preparing to kick.

I took the ball outside and kicked it against a wall, or I played in alleys and cul-de-sacs with my friends. If I learned any assertiveness as a child it was by asking a neighbour the inevitable question: "Can I get my ball, please."

As we grew up, my friends and I went further from home. We ran towards clear spaces and played with our ball. We ran and kicked until our legs were weary and no one wanted to collect the ball when it went behind the goal.

Occasionally my father took me to the football ground and I played on the club's training ground with local children. One day I was in the Oakwell boot-room with a friend of mine.

"Can we take the ball and kick it around?" asked my friend.

The Barnsley trainer assented. He assumed we were taking it across to the training ground. Instead we dashed on to Oakwell, took three or four penalties and came back.

I could say I had played on a League ground.

The trainer didn't look too pleased.

It wasn't something I could do regularly.

Oakwell was a sacred place, untarnished and poetic. I remember fairy-tale colours. The grass was green, our shirts were red and our shorts white. Their shirts were often white, their shorts black. Nothing fancy. Or so it seemed. In practice, some shirt colours were idiosyncratic, like the blue-and-white squares of Bristol Rovers or the bogey-green shirts of Plymouth Argyle, the first team I saw beat us. Our goalkeeper wore blue that day and became a different person.

Watching Barnsley from my seat high in the main grandstand, the action was doubly vicarious. My route to the players was via my father, and he suffered the helplessness of all managers – he couldn't kick a match ball till it had been used for 90 minutes. Oakwell was a beautiful place when we won home games, but something turned ugly one Saturday in December 1958. Sheffield Wednesday were our guests. I hated their blue-and-white pyjama-striped shirts and witch-like black shorts with white sash. Most of all I hated them winning and the way it happened on a dirty, muddy day which stained the hallowed colours.

A tackle on Johnny McCann fuelled my rage. My hero juggled the ball past the Wednesday full-back and then found arms wrestling with his neck. The two men tumbled to the ground. The crowd hooted and booed, and I picked up the mood helplessly. The full-back's dislocated shoulder seemed just reward, but what happened next seemed unfair. A Sheffield Wednesday goal, scored in injury-time, darkened the gloomy dusk still further and gave them a one-nil win.

I stared at Oakwell and it seemed a different place. I pictured myself in different parts of the ground. The green, velvet, comforting grass would never seem the same innocent colour again. The setting was tainted with mud and injury and the dingy twilight of a December day. The game was imbalanced. Perhaps Sheffield Wednesday would always win. Perhaps they were bigger. Perhaps they would be promoted to the First Division and my father's side relegated to the Third.

My golden feeling of childhood had been replaced by something more real.

The stark statistics show that there wasn't enough success to go round. In my father's early playing days, 88 clubs competed for four divisional Football League Championships and the only other major trophy was the FA Cup. It wasn't much, was it? All players must have had times when their dreams of a happy-ever-after script turned into something different.

1937

Tim was training on the Baseball Ground.

"Kick the ball over there," said one of the other players. "Over to that fellah."

"Him?" asked Tim, pointing to an old man walking round the touch-line with a fork. The man was in his sixties, not particularly tall, slightly stooped, his real physique concealed by baggy overalls. Tim kicked the ball towards him.

The man barely raised his leg but kicked the ball back without breaking stride.

So what? Tim was not overly impressed, but the other player smiled.

"Now you can tell your grandchildren that you played football with the great Steve Bloomer," he said.

Tim was starstruck now. He hadn't realised that England's record goalscorer was now working on the ground.

They changed in the home-team dressing-room at the Baseball Ground, their shirts (no numbers of course) hung out on pegs for them. Their routine was the same as the first-team routine. The man changing next to Tim was reading the newspaper.

"They've paid £7,000 for him, and he's playing against us today for the reserves."

"It's a lot of money to pay."

"Aye, he's a good player. We'll have to get rid of him early doors."

"Eh?" said Tim.

"We'll have to get the chopper out on him."

Tim carried on changing, not sure of how to take the conversation. Tim knew his team-mate was hard and experienced. They told a story about him playing at Old Trafford, how he walked to the touch-line to take a throw-in and the crowd wouldn't return the ball. "If you want it, you'll have to come and get it," they said, hating him. And, without further ado, he stepped over the wall and parted the packed crowd in a way that seemed impossible, so he could walk up the terracing, take the ball and walk back. He was hard. Experienced players knew that.

When it happened, about 30 minutes later, Tim was confused and surprised. He watched his team-mate go into a tackle, heard the solid thud, but his eyes had followed the ball. A cry of agony drew his attention to the player lying injured.

Trainers and the St John Ambulance men responded to the referee's whistle, and the opposition were reduced to ten men. An outlay of £7,000 suddenly looked a hopeful investment.

"He did the dirty on him," someone said.

1938

Albert Emptage was his name. Albert Emptage. Tim would remember it. The others talked about the redhead, name of Peter Doherty, but Tim, playing his third First Division game, would remember Albert Emptage. He would remember the name not because Albert Emptage was a famous international, but because he should have been marking Albert Emptage, and Albert Emptage was too good for him, much too good for him. Even the ordinary First Division players were good. Remember Albert Emptage.

Tim had a good look at Ernie Toseland, the Manchester City right winger, and could recognise him now – from the back. They said Toseland was probably the fastest player in the First Division. Tim hoped they were right.

Tim saw a bit of Peter Doherty too. Doherty beat so many players that day that Tim had to be one of them. Eric Keen, playing right-half, suffered more from Doherty though. A few weeks ago there had been a lot of bad publicity about Keen's appearance in a bankruptcy court. Against Doherty it was a different kind of bankruptcy.

At the Baseball Ground that day, Manchester City scored enough to declare.

Seven goals in all. It felt like more.

Humiliation. Embarrassment. Education.

Albert Emptage. Remember Albert Emptage.

The footballs were like concrete. Every week Tim played against someone who could kick the heavy ball like a cannonball and send it hurtling towards him, challenging him to choose between doing his duty and ducking. Free-kicks just outside the penalty area were the worst. Every week there was someone who could shoot harder than last week, and Tim would wake up on Sunday morning with imprints of the lace and the maker's name on his body. Many First Division newcomers went on to a pitch hoping they played well; Tim went out hoping Derby didn't concede a free-kick just outside their own penalty area. With players like Jack Nicholas they usually did.

And so it was at Brentford, on a rough, tough, bruising day when free-kicks were commonplace and Brentford were trying to hold on to their place at the top of Division One.

Brentford as Football League Champions? They were favourites in February 1938.

The ball was positioned for the free-kick, 20 yards from the Derby County goal. Tim felt he had a secure position in a wall of Derby County players: colossal Jack Barker on one side of him, hard man Jack Nicholas on the other. They held Tim by the arms and Tim could feel the strength of their muscular bodies. In a peculiar way, he felt proud. If only his friends in Cheltenham could see him now, next to these famous players.

A man wearing a red-and-white shirt took a mammoth run-up towards the round piece of leather concrete with a lace. To Tim the Brentford player seemed to run down the stand behind the goal, champing at the bit, and change from a distant dot to a Brentford Brobdingnag as he approached the stationary ball, ten yards from the wall of Derby County players. As the Brentford player thumped the ball, Tim felt himself propelled forward by the strong gripping arms of the two Jacks. Wham! The next thing he knew was the voice of the trainer: "Come on, yer big Nellie. There's nothing wrong with you."

Through the haze, trying to decide whether this Sunday would be spent with bruised ribs or a headache, Tim had some clear thoughts: "Why is it me who ends up on the floor? Did the two Jacks have a protective arm through mine, or did they have me in a half-nelson? Why does the ball always hit *me*?" Every week he thought about dodging a free-kick. Every week he dreaded another imprint from the ball and the prospect of visiting the Belper bonesetter they talked about at the club.

There was a feud that day at Brentford. Something had happened earlier in the season, that part of the season when Tim was in the reserves. Before the game Jack Barker remarked on what he was going to do. Tim didn't understand, but something odd was happening. For a start there were all the penalties. Brentford took the lead with a penalty, and Jack Barker was involved. Derby County equalised from a penalty, struck with typical power by Jack Nicholas. Derby County then scored a goal from open play before, on the hour, Brentford were awarded their second penalty. McKenzie made the score two-two.

After this third penalty of the match, close to the notorious soccer flash-point, halfway through the second half, the game erupted. Two Derby County players, Jack Barker and Reg Stockill, were cautioned by the referee. Then Jack Nicholas made a characteristically fierce tackle. The referee blew up and called together all the Derby County players except goalkeeper Jack Kirby, who was wrongly presumed to be a slow runner. The referee gave a guest lecture on fair play.

In the last minutes of the game, Ronnie Dix scored Derby's winning goal and Brentford's season was set to fall away.

Grimsby Town desperately needed a win to avoid relegation. The sight of Grimsby Town's half-back-line was enough to frighten anyone off their game. In football parlance they were known as "killers" who would kick the tops off football socks. With ten minutes to play, Grimsby winning two-one, a dismal crowd of less than 10,000 growing restless, Tim went into a tackle with one of the feared half-backs. Tim won the ball and sent it upfield. On the way back the experienced professional had a quiet word.

"Come here, young un," he said. "Now, slow down. Don't you know the arrangement?"

Tim didn't understand. When he thought about it later, he wondered if it had been said to make him think it was true. He didn't know.

Grimsby won two-one, and avoided relegation by two points.

Ninety per cent of the job was training. Dave Willis and Bill Bromage started the routine several weeks before the first match of the 1938-39 season. During the first week of pre-season training, the players were sent on a fast road walk of six or seven miles every morning. When they came back they ran two laps of the Baseball Ground track. Then they were put through a set of exercises by an army Physical Training instructor, the father of one of the young players at the club. They stretched their arms, cycled their legs and loosened joints in preparation for the next nine months.

In the afternoon the players lapped the track. They ran two laps, walked one, and so on. They lapped the track for about an hour, then did a few more exercises. For the first two weeks of pre-season training there was no sign of anything spherical. Then the players were told they were going to the Municipal Sports Ground. This meant they would finally see a ball. A chance to kick and head would be followed by a practice game. They were on their way.

Practice games, however, raised the competitive element. George Jobey brought his managerial presence to the touch-line and stood menacingly, dressed in suit and trilby hat, as the players dug deep in their psyches for good form. Jobey pointed his finger and told them what he thought: "I've seen washer-women play better than you lot... Hey, you... Yes, you... Get your hair cut... Don't wait till after the game, get it cut now."

Players would be sent to Waggie's during a game, the memory of George Jobey's threatening finger fresh in their minds for the whole season. A player with a dark complexion which called for two shaves a day might walk a long way round into the ground to avoid Jobey if he didn't feel totally clean-shaven. During one practice-match Reg Stockill tried an overhead kick which triggered Jobey's voice and finger. Words flowed ungenerously, the gist of them being that Jobey didn't think Stockill could see to kick the ball forward, let alone see through the back of his head.

"You!" Jobey might shout, capturing the attention of a field of footballers. "Come here." The poor athlete would make his way to the touch-line. "My wife can go faster than you," Jobey would say, his finger repeatedly stabbing the player in the chest.

The stubby forefinger would shift direction slightly as Jobey spoke but was always aimed at some part of the player being chastised. More than one player argued that Jobey's index finger was essential to his conversation. "Cut his arm off and he'd be struck dumb," one said, and a few fancied experimenting.

George Hannah was once asked by a trainer to explain the hole in the front of his training jumper. "Oh yes," Hannah said. "The manager did that the other day, when he was telling me how badly I played on Saturday." Even the trainer laughed.

Fifteen minutes before the end of training or before the end of a game, the groundsman filled the dressing-room baths with cold water and sprinkled in salts. The water was heated to boiling point by a steam pipe underneath the baths. "Get in there," Jobey told the players. "It's good for you. It'll do you good. And don't come out till I tell you to come out." The players dreaded defeats on an icy December day when a bath of scorching water stained their bodies and Jobey extended the torture. If Jobey stepped outside the dressing-room, one player would act as look-out while another ran cold water into the bath.

The big bath in the home-team dressing-room could seat about twenty. Very muddy players were under social pressure to visit the shower first. On a hot day, the groundsman would heat one bath and leave the other cold. The players could then move between dressing-rooms, first-teamers for once mixing with reserves as they sought the perfect temperature for their bodies, before drying their clean skins and rubbing olive oil into their hair.

Training was repetitive but Tim enjoyed most of it. Even the Wednesday morning sessions, one lap after another, until perhaps twenty laps had been chalked up. Later in the season, when the regular midweek games were over, Wednesday would mean a game of golf in the morning, lunch at the golf-club, and a second round of golf in the afternoon. It was better than persistent lapping. The players could hardly wait, even though a day's golfing meant coming in as early as nine o'clock.

Thursday morning training started with two or three laps to warm up. Then the players put on spiked shoes and prepared for half a dozen sprints the length of the field. One against one. This was the part Tim hated. When he had first arrived at Derby, spiked shoes were a new experience for him, and it took him a while to recover from that first ruse: "Go against Jack Kirby, son, He's a big lumbering goalkeeper." Yes, Jack Kirby looked clumsy, and he was only a goalkeeper after all, but he was a very fast awkward runner, as fast as Sammy Crooks himself.

By now Tim had found players of his own pace to run against. He was trying to improve his speed, but he was also learning that speed of thought was more important. If he could spot what was going to happen, then speed over five or six yards was what counted, not speed over fifty or a hundred. It was reassuring.

To make training equipment easier to manage, all the Derby County players were given a training number and a dressing-room peg. Tim's number was 21, which was free when he arrived. He had a locker labelled "21" and a rail in the drying-area with the same number. Like all the players, he had a place to hang his training clothes so they could be dry the next morning. Once a week his kit would be washed. His boots had "21" on the bottom, all his kit had the same number. By September 1938 it was appropriate to his age.

Tim had not yet grown accustomed to the idea of trusting his boots to someone else. When he first came to the club he would grab his boots after a game, ready to take them home. "Leave them there," he was told. With more experience he realised that his boots would be taken somewhere safe while he was in the bath, discreetly removed by "Old Jack", the cobbler. Jack was in his seventies and lived near the ground. On pay day, the players would give him something – sixpence or a shilling – and the old man was appreciated. Jack did his best to patch up old boots by putting pieces on them. Breaking in a new pair of boots was a fearful prospect – two months' work, even with trays of goose-grease to soften them. Players hated new boots. If Jack rescued old ones he was rewarded with a half-crown and a genuine look of worship.

Another Derby County supporter – let's call him Joe – was also appreciated by the players. They invited Joe on the annual outing to Burton-on-Trent. Before the evening practice-game, the players were shown round the town's breweries and then into the Bass Club in Guild Street. Tim noticed men playing snooker for money.

After a few minutes, having sized up the strength of the players, Sammy Crooks stood up, and spoke with typical forwardness: "Me and my mate will play any two in the place."

Two Burtonians accepted the offer. Sammy Crooks took Joe by the hand and led him to the table. A coin was tossed, then Sammy took a cue and broke the pattern of the snooker balls. The first opponent ran up a break of more than twenty and retired to his seat with a smug smile on his face. Joe stepped up and cleared the table. Tim's eyes popped out of his head. He had never seen snooker played like that. Joe, of course, was a champion (Joe Davis) and Sammy Crooks knew what he was doing.

Mixing with top-class professionals from other sports suggested to Tim that he was at the top of his own profession. The coming season offered a rich vein of promise. No longer were those early dreams of international caps, League Championships and FA Cup medals totally unrealistic. There was a measure of possibility. Some sages were tipping Derby County for the League Championship, and, as it turned out, they were fair judges.

One week Tim faced a man known in the business as "a box of tricks". The next week it might be "a speed merchant", one who could "catch pigeons". Tim's preference was to mark speedy players because they weren't running all the time. The "box of tricks" was always looking for the ball and was capable of making a wing-half look a complete novice.

They warned Tim about Ronnie Starling of Aston Villa. Starling played at inside-left rather than inside-right, but Tim was warned anyway. "Watch him, Tim," they said, which was really helpful. Starling had one very unusual trick. Running towards the touch-line with the ball at his feet, facing the terraces, apparently out of danger, he could suddenly cross one leg over the other and backheel a centre, the ball whistling over a startled defender's shoulder into the goalmouth.

On the second Saturday of the 1938-39 season, Tim faced Starling and the rest of Aston Villa's costly team, recently promoted from the Second Division. Tim had been to Villa Park with Cheltenham Town Reserves three years ago. This time he was looked after in First Division style: tea in the dressing-room at half-time, tea and lemonade at full-time. The warmer the weather, the more the lemonade, and this was only just September. After the match, Tim got in the bath with his tea and thought about how far he had come. Nothing like an overawing four-one defeat today. He was part of a winning team and had played his part. After "towelling himself dry", he sat, drank lemonade, worked out how the League table would look. Two wins and a draw in the first three games meant five points. It was a good start. It was the start a Championship team would make.

Derby County's fifth game of that exciting 1938-39 season was Sunderland at home, one of the toughest of the season's forty-two. If they won this one they would be amongst the leaders. As Ambulance men looked after fainting victims on the packed Popular side of the Baseball Ground, Tim faced the sun and prepared to mark Raich Carter. Derby centre-forward Harry Travis kicked off.

Action quickly moved to the Sunderland right wing, the ball disappeared in and out of play, reached Raich, who created some room and shot from long range, into the crowd. Tim responded, started a move between Ronnie Dix and Dai Astley, on to Jimmy Hagan and against the crossbar. Derby attacked the Sunderland goal, Johnny Mapson saved, Harry Travis closed in to communicate, shoulder to shoulder, and Mapson felt bruises coming. A few minutes later Travis moved in again on Mapson, but Sunderland centre-half George Johnston spoke with his own shoulder and Travis felt the bumps.

Mapson saved again, Travis challenged, Johnston protected and the Derby crowd took umbrage. A black kitten strayed on to the pitch, restored the calm, needed catching. Raich Carter had a shot at the Derby goal, the ball went wide. Johnston grazed the grass with more tackles, fouled Travis, wrestled him to the ground, the crowd booed. Johnston appeared to stop Ronnie Dix's shot with his hands, the referee waved play on, the crowd booed. Raich Carter tried a header at the Derby goal, the ball went wide. Johnston and Travis committed several more fouls, the referee spoke to them, the crowd booed. Dally Duncan was pulled up for offside, the crowd booed. Elsewhere pandemonium. Sunderland players surrounded Travis, Johnston reeled around clutching his face, the crowd booed again.

The referee separated the players and investigated. He had seen nothing. The linesman on the Derby right wing had also seen nothing. Short of calling in a forensic scientist to examine the blood on Travis's hand and the gap in Johnston's teeth, the referee could do little. He could act only on what he saw, or what a linesman saw. He spoke to all the players and dropped the ball back into play around the edge of the Sunderland penalty area.

Two minutes from the end, Johnston headed out a long centre from Jack Nicholas. Ronnie Dix urgently kicked the ball from 20 yards, past Mapson, between the goal-posts, into "the onion bag". It was the only goal of the game.

Harry Travis missed the next game with a poisoned hand. He never played for the first team again, even after discarding his sling. He already had four free transfers on his record. The fifth took him to Tranmere Rovers.

Arsenal at Highbury. *The* Arsenal. Winning one-nil. Standing on the edge of the penalty area, watching a two-person game that was about to begin – Derby goalkeeper Frank Boulton against Arsenal penalty-taker Cliff Bastin. And Tim's childhood friend, Cedric, was watching too, high in the Highbury stand, no doubt remembering his own one-against-one games against Tim on Fox Fields. Nobody had watched Cedric and Tim play their version of Arsenal against Derby County, but thirty thousand watched Cliff Bastin taking a penalty against Frank Boulton.

But Tim wondered what was happening: "Why is Frank standing there?"

Frank Boulton stood close to the right-hand post. Bastin could pick his spot from the space on the goalkeeper's right. Up he came. Kicked the ball. Straight at Frank

Boulton, who bent down, gathered the ball, smiled. A penalty save in only his sixth game for Derby County. His previous club was Arsenal.

Sammy Crooks made a goal for Dally Duncan and Derby County won two-one.

Reality was stealing scripts from Tim's dreams.

They drew at Grimsby, scored five against Stoke, beat Blackpool and won at Brentford. The 11th game of the season, at Birmingham, looked easy, for a team in such good form. Birmingham were near the bottom, and the Derby lads were confident: "If they win the toss they'll want to kick the same way as us."

It was mid-October, and Prime Minister Neville Chamberlain had just sealed an agreement at Munich which promised "peace in our time". The mood was euphoric, jubilant, and now they thought the season would go the distance. Derby players could safely put all their energies into League games.

Birmingham fans were not so elated. "War's a terrible thing," grumbled one, "but it's the only thing that could save our team from relegation."

Birmingham three, Derby County none.

Only the uncertainty was certain.

On the last Saturday of October 1938, Derby County went top of the First Division after 13 games. Their two-nil victory at Chelsea was threatened only by an encroaching London fog during the last 20 minutes of the game. The team travelled back by train. Jack Barker, the Derby captain, approached Tim on St Pancras station.

"What are you earning, Tim?" Jack said.

Tim told him.

"You should be on top money," the captain remarked. "Have a chat with the Boss."

"Pardon."

"Have a chat with the Boss."

Tim thought about it between London and Derby. At Derby railway station Jack Barker came up again.

"Go on, Tim, have a chat with the Boss. He's in a jovial mood. We're top of the League. It's a good chance. Go on."

Tim walked cautiously towards George Jobey, who looked merry on port and points.

"Er, excuse me, Boss… You see, I've played a lot of games in the first team. Do you think I should be on first-team money?"

George Jobey didn't repeat himself in the next five minutes. "Just because you're *in the first team* doesn't mean that you're *a first-team player*. You'll get first-team wages *when* you're a first-team player. Getting big-headed won't get you very far. Wait until you can play before you approach me again."

Tim stood on the platform and listened to different words but more of the same. He walked away deflated.

Three days later he collected his wages from Billy Moore, the club secretary.

"I think you've overpaid me, Mr Moore," said Tim.

"No, no, that's right," said Billy Moore. "The Boss has put you on first-team wages."

Tim's new wage was the maximum of £8 per week, plus plenty of bonuses – £2 for a win and £1 for a draw. A good run in the FA Cup might increase the bonuses still further. If they won the Cup Final they would receive £8 a man, though a draw in the Final was worth the same as in a League game – a pound apiece. All the same, it was good money. If Derby County won the League and Tim stayed in the team, he would earn more than Raich Carter, more than Stanley Matthews, more than Eddie Hapgood, more than most British footballers.

George Jobey brought in the new player and introduced him: "I'm sure you all know Dave McCulloch here. We've just signed him from Brentford."

The transfer fee was £10,000.

It could only help their quest for the Championship. Especially now they were top of the League.

Tim sat alone on a seat at St Pancras Station, rested his head in his hands and wallowed after defeat in the 15th game. "What had gone wrong?" he thought. "We shouldn't have been beaten by Charlton Athletic. Alright, they have a good defence – only two goals conceded in seven games – and they're just below us in the League, but we shouldn't have lost. Dave McCulloch was a bit quiet today. What did one of the others say? Because he'd played for Scotland during the week."

He looked up as a shadow fell across him. George Jobey, smart in his suit and trilby-hat, fresh from a couple of drinks, finger itching to point, stood before him. Jobey was not very tall, but cast a large shadow.

"What's the matter with you?" Jobey asked.

There was no reply. Tim's miserable face said it all.

"Look, I'll tell you something," said Jobey. "If you can't learn to lose in this game you never deserve to win."

Elland Road at the end of November, and Tim was once again staggered by Sammy Crooks. He thought he knew Sammy now, thought he understood his style on the field. He knew, for instance, that Sammy wanted the ball passed into his stride rather than to his feet. And he had seen that unique trick of Sammy's a hundred times. How did he do it? Sammy ran towards a full-back at top speed with the ball at his feet, head over the ball, legs scampering along, his right leg suddenly shaping to the ball to kick a long cross. For every inch of the movement it was certain that Sammy was hammering the ball into the centre. But he would chip it lightly, no more than a touch, drag the ball back with his left foot and sprint past the full-back on the outside. Once clear, Sammy Crooks could not be caught by anyone in the world. He was a gust of wind with incredible speed, perfect balance and the confidence to try anything.

Tim knew he was fast, but didn't know how fast.

Leeds United's Tom Holley strolled across from his central position to collect an easy ball. Sammy zipped across the ground like a motor-bike leaving a built-up area, snatched the ball from Holley's feet, took it past him, crossed it, congratulated the scorer.

For once Tim didn't watch the ball. He looked at Tom Holley. He'd never seen a footballer in such a state of shock.

"It's no wonder we're top of the League," Tim thought.

After the four-one win, Sammy was irrepressible. "I've had a letter from the FA asking me to stop my body-swerve," he said. "Apparently when I did it at Birmingham the other week, two express trains ran off the lines."

Tim was in love with his workplace. It was more than just a football ground, more than simply "the Baseball". In everyday speech it was *the ground.* The players talked about it all the time.

"See you down the ground, lads."

"They want you down the ground."

"Are you stopping down the ground?"

During the week the players lived and worked in a relatively enormous space, a site that could have housed hundreds. On alternate Saturdays the club threw the best parties in town. Paying guests turned up for a good time, and their hosts did their best to entertain and succeed. Tim grew to recognise people in the crowd. Together they grew older by the fortnight, some of them men his own age who he stood near when waiting to collect the ball and take a throw-in. They were dressed for winter, he was not, but he was warmer than them. He could hear them call his name:

"Are we going to win, Tim?"

"Come on, Tim, get them going."

It was a friendly atmosphere, but he knew he was accountable to the supporters. He played, they judged. On the whole it was a good football crowd at Derby – all the professionals said that. But the pitch wasn't up to much. You needed wellingtons with a long stud in winter and farming gear in spring. As the pitch was some feet below sea-level, it was especially bad after heavy rain, when reporters enjoyed exercising their imaginations. The pitch was "a duck-pond", "a Mississippi swamp", "a mussel-bed", "a quagmire", "a sea of treacle" and "a snakes-and-ladder board". But it was also bad at the back end of the season. By then it was bone hard, furrowed and grassless, and Jack Howe often said that it was easier to control the ball on the terraces.

The spectators, too, grumbled about conditions, except when their team played well and won. Then they would celebrate, and those who could afford it would call in at the market-hall to buy presents for their families. More so as December came and Christmas beckoned. Seven wins, two draws and no defeats was a good home record. It was Championship form.

Then came Middlesbrough on 17 December. Very strange. A third of spectators were missing, presumed Christmas shopping. A few Derby County players weren't there, presumed injured or out of form. And Tim learned a cliché: "You can only play as well as the other team lets you."

Middlesbrough had Mickey Fenton, Benny Yorston, Wilf Mannion, plenty of shots, the right mood, a good team. Fenton hit a goal-post twice in the first 10 minutes and it got worse. When Middlesbrough led four-one, Tim counted their players. Just to make sure.

Nine… ten… eleven.

It seemed more.

"This fellah Mercer will be bringing it through today," said Jack Nicholas to Ronnie Dix, Derby's inside-left.

Tim looked across the dressing-room at Jack Nicholas and something fell into place. So top-class wing-halves like Joe Mercer of Everton could force inside-forwards to watch them. It had never occurred to Tim. Now he looked again at Jack Nicholas. More warily. He wasn't sure he really wanted to share the same piece of mud as strong tacklers like Jack. It was well-known that the Derby right-half didn't miss many games with injury. Less well-known was how many opponents did.

Tim's job with Derby County Football Club was geared towards bursts of 45-minute activity when he was expected to restrict an opposing inside-forward. Ideally, he won the ball and then passed it to a nearby colleague. He was raw enough to believe that the ball was best won by tackling rather than intercepting. He was also naive enough to think that attacking should be left solely to forwards.

When Tim won the ball he had a number of options, depending on his position on the pitch. He always thought in terms of passing it to someone, passing it quickly, to someone unmarked or on the move. In front of him were five international forwards – Crooks, Astley, McCulloch, Dix and Duncan – so Tim felt confident that they wouldn't trip over the ball if he gave it to any of them. Even when he was in a good position to take the ball forward, to bring it through in Joe Mercer's style, he looked for someone to pass it to. A strange attitude perhaps for a player who had started as an outside-right and centre-forward, but an attitude dictated by the calibre of players around him. He couldn't do much better than pass the ball directly to Dally Duncan's feet.

Dally Duncan had tricks. He could turn on a sixpence. He teased a full-back until the full-back was off-balance and facing the touch-line crowd; then, twisting to his right, ball glued to his left foot, Duncan would swivel clockwise, through 270 degrees, and glide along the touch-line. Not once but a dozen times each game. His control in his left foot was so good that he escaped being clobbered, even though he put himself between the ball and the defender while he was turning. He made mugs of right full-backs. He dillied and dallied, just like the song said, but when he turned and moved, everything happened quickly. He was almost all left foot, but it was a wonderful left foot.

Duncan did for Everton on the Baseball Ground. He turned on a sixpence and turned the game, a vital game between the First Division's top two teams. He pirouetted clockwise, side-stepped, twisted away from his inadequate single marker and slid along the touch-line. And then came Dally's other party-piece – the ridiculous shot from the wing. The ball swirled and swerved and baffled Everton goalkeeper Ted Sagar. Tim was the first across the heavy pitch to shake Dally's hand, the last to know the winger's real name was Douglas.

Successful footballers were a captivating collection of men, laughing and smiling, story-telling and teasing, fit and lithe, male models of good deportment, neat and well-manicured from their daily baths and wearing the latest in eye-catching clothing from the best tailors in town. One Derby County player bought a new suit with every win bonus.

One wintry day at the height of success, George Wilcox, Les Bailey and Tim went to Jackson the tailor, where they all bought plus-fours and accessories. Back at Mrs Smith's they felt like film stars. In their landlady's lounge, the players paraded new suits and socks – a collection of small and large checks – with heavy shoes that were ideal for the golf-course on Wednesdays.

Mrs Smith's lounge had a high fireplace with bars across. The coal was usually stacked high. George Wilcox stood with his back to the fire, reading a newspaper. The others sniffed the air.

"Can you smell burning?" someone asked.

"Probably some old rags Mrs Smith put on the fire."

No one thought much about it, but the smell lingered.

"Yes, I can smell it now," said George. He turned round and touched the plus-fours at the back of his legs where the material puffed out. Two charred pieces fell on the floor.

They laughed like fairground clowns.

They could afford to laugh. Not only were they relatively rich, but Derby County were five points clear at the top of the First Division, and New Year's Eve fell on the best day of the week for celebration, a Saturday.

1939

Sunderland away. Early in January. A grey, cheerless afternoon, brightened only by the firefly-like appearances of people lighting cigarettes and pipes. Miserable weather during a miserable economic depression. There was straw on the pitch and the usual Roker wind. At half-time, unemployed demonstrators carried banners along the touch-line (until the police took them away). Then fog rolled in from the sea, and the wind failed to blow it away from the pitch. Finally there was impending darkness, spectators shut off from the closing minutes of the game.

Not a nice day. And Sunderland won one-nil. Raich Carter was not winning medals every year but he could still play.

Tim felt something slipping away when they went to Blackpool in February. He realised they were running out of players. Jack Barker was injured, Sammy Crooks was missing games with injuries and full-back Jack Howe was injured too. But what baffled him was the transfer of Dai Astley to Blackpool. It didn't make sense. Dai Astley and Ronnie Dix were pals, they played well *together*. Why transfer one? "It must have been something to do with money," Tim thought. He didn't really understand.

They were hanging on, but only just.

One Thursday afternoon, early in March, 1939, Tim lay in the bath on his own after home to Chelsea. It was the third home defeat in succession, and Tim knew that wasn't good enough to win a Championship, even if the Baseball Ground had been covered with pools of water for the Chelsea game.

He heard one trainer talking to another: "We had one player yesterday who never passed a ball to one of his own players all afternoon."

Alone in the bath, Tim found himself listening to the trainer. "Is it me they're talking about?" he wondered. "It could be."

He sunk deeper in the bath and considered what he could do about it. He came up with a resolution. He would try to go through a game without giving the ball to the opposition. He began to think deeply about the means and ways of passing a ball perfectly. Don't give away the ball. Never give it away.

The pitch was an exposed place with nowhere to hide – not from George Jobey, the trainers, team-mates or spectators. You couldn't linger over a tea-break or sneak away into a corner; someone would notice you. Tim knew that while he was out there, playing wing-half, he would have to work.

He learned by watching other players. Nobody called him on one side to talk about football. Nobody told him how to improve his game. Nobody suggested that he should occasionally try a shot. Players were congratulated, encouraged, bawled out and chastised, but nobody explained the details.

"Why am I in the second team this week, Boss?" asked one player dropped from the first team.

"Because the third team haven't got a game," replied Jobey.

Tim knew that he would have to do his own thinking about this complex game. You had to assess the condition of the pitch, the strength of the wind, the bounce of the ball and, above all, the movement of the players and the right pass. In future, when trying to pass the ball accurately, he would construct an imaginary line on the pitch, and assess his terrain like a golfer on a putting-green. The techniques were similar after all. Golfers, like wing-halves, had to drive, chip and pass a ball, except that their ball and target were stationary. In soccer the hole shifted as a team-mate moved, and the ball bounced and spun. It didn't worry Tim. He would just try harder. Perfect passing became his fad and he loved everything to do with it.

If they chased the League Championship again, in future years, he would be better prepared. He would be ready. He wouldn't be so innocent. And, sure enough, that time did come… but that's a later chapter in this story.

Ten minutes before kick-off, George Jobey walked into the Derby County dressing-room. Could this be a team talk? Could it be an attempt to inject motivation and inspiration into his declining team? Could it be a finger-pointing exercise to instil fear. The players waited for his words.

"There's someone wanting a word with you," said Jobey. Then he left the team in the hands of another man, a surrogate manager who had a message of his own.

"Whatever happens today, you're on the bonus," he said. "Now, what's your answer?"

Tim tried to understand. The opposition needed points, and this man was from the opposition. Tim thought he should be incensed at what he was hearing. He wasn't sure. He waited to study his team-mates' reactions.

"No," said one of the other young players.

"No," said one of the older players.

"Just a minute," said another older man. "I'm captain here. Just leave it to me, Sir."

The surrogate manager nodded approvingly, thanked the captain, and left the dressing-room.

A few of the Derby County team turned on their captain.

"What did you do that for?" they asked.

"Why be so bloody stupid?" the captain replied. "Whatever happens we get the bonus. Let's go out and do them if we can."

Derby County paid the bonuses.

The story about Les Bailey frightened Tim. Les was offered £6 in the summer, £6 during the season and £8 if he was in the first team, a pay scale known as "the sliding scale". Les had played almost half the games that season, the 1938-39 season, deputising for the injured Jack Barker. He thought he should be guaranteed £8 per week, first team or not.

"This contract," said Les, when he approached George Jobey in the manager's office. "It's no good to me."

"What do you mean 'no good'?"

"I'm not signing for that."

"You're not?"

"No."

Jobey picked up the contract, tore it into pieces and threw the bits into his wastepaper bin.

Les Bailey was out of work. He had to move on.

He went back to Worksop to look for a job and eventually signed for Llandudno Town.

6. Origins of a Football Family

One time, when I was very small, a teacher asked us to bring our favourite Christmas present to school. I went in wearing mine: a red shirt with white collar and sleeves, knee-length white shorts, red and white hooped socks, and football boots.

The teacher was so impressed she sent me to show the headmaster. The girl in the nurse's uniform came with me.

In March 1957 I transferred from pencil to ink in school lessons. I know this for a fact because we wrote diaries during English lessons that season and I still have mine. I wrote in pseudo-reportage with bad spelling about games involving Barnsley or Barnsley Reserves: "On Saturday I went to the football match. Barnsley beat Grimsby 2-0. The first one came in the 77th minute when De Grunchie handed the ball and Kaye slamed the penalty kick past Williams. Then Kaye put Barnsley further ahead one minute from time when he drove the ball past a croud of players. On Sunday I went to Sunday Shool."

In my diary I recorded my first attempts at playing football. Sometimes the games were against my father in our driveway, and I soon developed an ability to turn defeats into friendlies and wins into League games. Games with my father were usually friendlies.

On Wednesday afternoons we were shepherded to the school playing-field to play football. I played on the left-wing, where I mimicked John McCann as much as possible, so much so that the other boys eventually nicknamed me "Stylo". I learned that the left wing was a pleasant, reflective position from which to observe play. I always noticed who scored our goals, and I recorded the details in my diary, even when the game finished eleven-goals apiece, as it did one Wednesday in November.

In my diary I confessed to creating my own football programmes and football coupons. I put a lot of work into programmes for fictitious games like "Boys v Cars" and "Bunny Town against the Board eleven". They were usually FA Cup games. "I am making alsorts of programmes," I wrote in late-September.

I also produced my own sports paper ("The White One") which contained reports and profiles from my fantasy world of football. I usually played centre-forward for "Boys" and the classic lead story had me carried off on a stretcher with a head injury before coming back to score the two late goals that gave us the four-three win. One was sure to be a brave diving header.

My 1956-57 diary, therefore, oscillated between match reports, programmes, fictional newspapers, Cup draws, football pools, references to television programmes like "Sports Special" and comments on literature like Charles Buchan's "Soccer Gift Book" and "Raich Carter's Soccer Star". Inspired by David H Brown, I kept a Barnsley scrapbook, although in my diary I often called it a "scarp book". With my friends, I played games like magnetic football, Penalty, New Footy and Blow Football, always inventing enough teams for a League.

Otherwise, I didn't bother much with football.

My father would sometimes look at my home-made newspapers or read my diary.

"You've got good handwriting," he said once. "I bet you'll get a job using your handwriting one day."

I sat near Pamela in class. We swopped our comics and shared our secrets. She had a furry animal toy called Tiddles which she brought round to our house.

At school one day Pamela asked me what I wanted for Christmas.

"A Denis Compton Annual," I told her. "It's all about football and cricket."

Sometimes, though, the boys called each other "sissies" if they were spotted talking to girls. A conversation with a girl could be turned into something confusing and embarrassing. There were other things that boys should do instead, like fishing and fighting and football.

I passed my eleven-plus at nine and left primary school a year early. My parents seemed pleased but I was disappointed. The primary-school headmaster said I had been a cert to play outside-left in the school team the following year, and my new school, at Wakefield, played rugby rather than soccer.

My parents bought me a reversible rugby jersey. One side was amber-and-black hoops, the other plain blue. The shorts were dark blue. I didn't like the colours. Too jazzy. No football team would wear colours like that.

I tried to learn new skills, like running with a ball in my hands and throwing my arms round the waist of a boy on the run.

Kicking goals was easy enough.

Playing soccer in the playground at break was even easier.

One day, my father collected me from my new school at Wakefield. We drove through to Leeds to watch a game. As we collected our tickets, a man came out of the Leeds United office. He chatted to my father.

"Is this your son?" he asked.

"Yes, this is my son – Andrew."

My father turned to me.

"This is Don Revie," he said.

Don Revie offered his hand. I put out mine. Unfortunately I'd been playing rugby at school and hadn't had time for a shower. My hand was caked with mud.

Another occasion, at Oakwell, I became infatuated with the Leyton Orient outside-left. It was probably because his name was Andrews and I imagined that he faintly resembled my Uncle Bill. I wanted the winger to be called Bill Andrews, but my programme told me that his name was Jimmy. As we slipped to defeat, I retained a curious detachment. The game was going against us, but I was salvaging something from defeat. I was thinking about all my relatives called Andrews.

Perhaps those early thoughts were my first recognition of the complex origins of football families. Footballers establish themselves as professionals because of how they grow up and who they marry. Sometimes an insecurity in their background lights a fire of ambition and anger which is channelled into physical energy. Other times, a secure upbringing gives them the space to experiment and search for extremes in what they can do. Usually it is a perverse combination of the two.

While researching this book, I was intrigued by various branches of the Andrews family, but my attention was particularly caught by Peter Andrews, one of the world's first professional footballers, if not the *world's first.*

In the early 1870s, Peter Andrews lived in Slatefield Street, Glasgow, and worked as an insurance agent. He was playing for Eastern at Barrowfield Park until his move south, in 1876, to Sheffield, then England's hotbed of soccer. One source suggests that, although he was the first Scot to play football in England, he did not move specifically to play football: "The Scottish firm by whom he was employed sent him to Leeds on business, and after he had been there for some months he became connected with the Heeley club." The same source refers to James Lang as the first Scot to cross the border specifically to play football.

Other sources do not separate between these two early Scottish footballers: "Andrews and Lang, having paid visits to Lancashire and Yorkshire in the many matches played between Scotch and English clubs, saw in Sheffield...better opportunities for work at higher wages than they could get at home."

Jimmy Catton, football's earliest sage, is usually a reliable source: "It is said that they had gone to Sheffield to fulfil situations, but their occupation chiefly consisted of playing football and reading the sporting periodicals of the day."

In Sheffield, Peter Andrews lived on Gleadless Road, Heeley, and his neighbours were Gibson the machine-ruler and Bowles the butcher. A local directory gives his occupation as "agent for Scottish Legal Insurance Co."

When he returned to Glasgow from Sheffield he lived on Dalmarnock Road and worked as a cashier at WC Scott & Co, Greenhead's oil and soap factory.

The 1878-79 Scottish Football Annual describes his play: "a hard-working forward...with good speed and endurance, though too excited at goal."

Reports of matches added to my knowledge of his style:

"Andrews ran the ball up the western side of the field."

"Andrews made several capital runs."

"Andrews shot in quickly."

"Andrews played it cleverly through."

"Andrews delighted the crowd with his dribbling."

"Andrews came in with a rush and it rebounded from him through the goal."

Recently, I visited the area of Glasgow where Peter Andrews grew up, intent on discovering more about his life. But I didn't need to. As soon as I arrived in Bridgeton, I made the connection with John McCann. Although separated by eighty years, both were left-footed, left-sided forwards who had learned their football in Bridgeton before departing to earn a living in South Yorkshire. I can imagine Peter Andrews jinking along the left wing like Johnny McCann, and I wouldn't want to spoil my image by learning more.

On that trip to Glasgow, I walked across Glasgow Green, where a man can watch several football games without straying too far. I saw goal-posts made of litter bins, iron posts, sweaters and track-suits. I watched a one-a-side game in a cage built on four brick walls, and a more expansive game which involved seventeen children, all in replica shirts, with intermittent fights. I also saw a father giving kicking practice to his son of three or four.

I felt I had found part of my spiritual home, where the earliest professional footballers had learned their trade and where my first hero, John McCann, had learned his skills. In that moment I pictured myself as an indirect descendant of an extended Andrews family, a community of wage-earners who depended on professional football for love and lucre.

The 1920s

There was nothing legal about the adoption. The boy knew that. He was eternally grateful that Bill and Eunice Andrews had welcomed him into their family, allowed him to call them Mum and Dad and raised him alongside their three sons and any of the nephews who resided at the Briars from time to time.

The Andrews boys were raised on the natural resources of bucolic Charlton Kings, a hamlet three miles and over 300 houses from the centre of Cheltenham. When the thistles grew tall in May they all went thistle-cutting. In June the boys stalked cowslip fields, plucking yellow flowers to sell to men who made cowslip wine. At haymaking time they all went haymaking. They collected acorns for the pigman, wild walnuts for themselves and mushrooms to be cooked by their mother. They picked plums from their own garden, scrumped apples and pears from various orchards, collected sloes and crab-apples, and, in September and October, cut the pockets out of their jackets and filled the linings with wild hazelnuts. In autumn they waded in blackberries. The eldest boy, Bill, cycled to Poole's in Cheltenham High Street with a dozen pounds of blackberries perched awkwardly on his bicycle handlebars, juice dripping to the ground by the end of his journey. In winter the boys collected firewood from the woods, and stacked it into a box fitted with old bicycle wheels, hoping the wheels wouldn't buckle too much on the return journey. And, at Christmas, they joined the queue outside East Court, the Gresham residence, where carol singing was as profitable as anywhere.

The Andrews family worked the extensive garden rather than the outhouses of the Briars. They kept ducks and chickens, and reared two pigs a year – one called "Easter", the other "Christmas" – and when they killed them they ate everything, from chops to chitterlings. The garden was bordered by bee-hives on one side, the houses of Nelmes Row on the other, and, at the bottom, where the ground dropped sharply and a nightingale sang daily, the cool waters of a brook which offered healing powers. If a boy bruised his leg playing football he could stand in the brook and let the water lap against his leg. When he felt fit he could step over the brook and run on to the hills, ready to find a patch to play football. There was no shortage of space.

The family lived from day to day, attuned to subtle seasonal changes, rushing to the door with mugs to buy elvers when the men brought round the produce of the Severn Bore. They were a rural, country-wise family, confident in their environment, self-sufficient, disciplined by climate and their father's boxing-gloves, their household dominated by males: even the Alsatian dog was "George". Their locale was the picturesque, undulating scenery of Gloucestershire greenery and Cotswold stone. No slag heaps and pit dust. No urban, industrial sprawl. There was no subculture that shouted professional football, just a low-key masculine interest in physical activity and the need for siblings to play together. The adopted Andrews boy joined in. He had been Christened Victor Timothy but a school-teacher looked at the unmelodic combination of names and murmured disapprovingly. "Surely, that's not right," the teacher said. "It must be Timothy Victor." So the names were changed round, and the boy didn't question it. Everyone called him Tim.

He joined the Andrews family when he was very young, too young to have memories of his previous life, old enough to have been affected. He retained his original surname, something that kept him apart from the other Andrews boys, a residue which troubled him enormously. But on the football field there were no introductions, no surnames, so the boy called Tim, an adopted Andrews brother, secure and insecure in his family roots, belonging and separate, learned to love the team nature of sport. The word sport seduced him, possessed him, obsessed him. Boxing, running, cricket, football, any of these, he was first in the queue, and especially football.

The Briars, home of the Andrews family, was a cramped, cosy, two-storey house with a corrugated iron roof. Uncle Percy made the house look small. He stood in front of the coal-fire or sat on the settee – no one sat at the piano, no one could play it – and told stories about his days as a professional boxer. He told the boys how he and his boxing friends toured fair-booths inviting spectators to go three rounds after a stooge had set an example. Uncle Percy couldn't resist demonstrating a few left jabs and right hooks.

"Watch the pewter and the willow pattern, Uncle Percy."

"Aye, and don't knock Queen Victoria off the wall."

"Boxing is all a matter of body work," explained Uncle Percy. The boys looked at the boxing-gloves that hung over the door. When they misbehaved their father put on one pair, forced the culprit into another and the winner was never in doubt. The boys longed for any strategy to use against their father, so they listened attentively as Uncle Percy spoke: "It's all a matter of body work. You don't need to use your hands. Just sway from side to side to avoid punches."

"How do you mean, Uncle Percy?"

"I'll show you. I'll put a handkerchief on the floor and make a bet with you. I'll stand with my feet on one side of the handkerchief and you have to stand with yours on the other side of the handkerchief, and I bet you won't be able to lay a finger on me."

"Impossible."

"We're bound to hit him if we're standing on the same handkerchief."

The boys – three Andrews and one adopted – would have bet anything on it. They bet what they had and waited. Uncle Percy took out his handkerchief and walked to the door that led from the living-room to the kitchen. The door was nearly as wide as high, so Uncle Percy had plenty of space as he bent to place the handkerchief on the floor in the doorway.

"Now, stand on that side of the handkerchief," he said to one of the boys.

The boy obliged. Uncle Percy shut the door and stood on the other side of the handkerchief.

"I bet you can't hit me," he shouted through the closed door.

1929

Charlton Kings, Cheltenham. An 11-year-old boy was embarrassed by his new clothes: a gaudy shirt of red, yellow and black hoops; shorts an immaculate white; and new football boots. It was his first time in football boots and he remembered the shopkeeper's puzzling words: "These are Steve Bloomer boots. Steve Bloomer. Derby County and England."

As the boy walked unsteadily out of the Andrews house, he wondered how an adult like Steve Bloomer could fit into boots so small. Steve Bloomer must have had very small feet, the boy deduced. That was the only explanation.

He walked towards school, in good time for the afternoon session. His route was inundated with football pitches. First he crossed the main London Road, which was ideal for winter five-a-side games played with a tennis-ball, touch-lines marked by kerbs. London Road was a floodlit pitch, lit by the lamp outside the Andrews house. The only drawback was the need for portable goal-posts, such as dustbins, which could be nonchalantly moved if an occasional car or Black-and-White bus rattled and chugged along the road. London was 90 miles away, an extra-terrestrial journey for 11-year-old boys in the late 1920s.

The biggest threat to winter floodlit games came from the local police constable, who patrolled his beat on foot. Making an arrest meant a three-mile journey into Cheltenham – at best by public tram – so the policeman dealt with miscreants on the spot, often giving lads a clip around the ear. "Don't let me catch you playing football in the street again," he yelled at the boys. "You'll be for it if you're playing here tomorrow night when I come round." Then he would lower his voice and add with a noncommittal half-cocked smile, his eyes laughing, "That'll be at eight o'clock." And the players then knew when to take half-time.

Having crossed London Road, the boy dodged down Duke's Alley at the side of the Duke of York public house. The solid leather of the boots and the positioning of the nails warned him of blisters ahead. He turned right into East End Road, known to him as the Back Lane. This was a summer football pitch; it was quiet enough in winter too – only three or four cars a day – but had no street lamps. For once, he resisted the appeal of the red-brick walls near Wager Court. Normally he tested their compliance at returning tennis-balls, kicked right-footed on the way to school, left-footed on the way home. Today, his new football boots felt too cumbersome, too conspicuous.

A few minutes later he walked through iron gates into the playground of Charlton Kings Boys' School, on to yet another football pitch. Strangely, though, despite his football kit, he felt out of place on all his usual football pitches. He was too aware of his different clothes.

The legend of a former headmaster, the frightening "Boss" Fry, still lingered in the school. The boys must conform. Yet, dressed in a loud shirt with red, yellow and black hoops, walking noisily into his afternoon lesson wearing Steve Bloomer football boots, the boy knew his clothes didn't match those of the rest of his class. He also remembered being caned for playing football in the wrong place.

The teacher came in to stress the three R's – reading, writing and 'rithmetic – and dictate a few lines for the boys to copy down. They would not leave the classroom until a hand-bell was heard. All except one boy. For on this afternoon, before the end of the lesson, another teacher interrupted and spoke to the teacher in charge:

"Have you got one of the football team in here?"

As he left his seat, the boy felt his red, yellow and black shirt scream at his class-mates. Self-consciously, he walked towards the door, wondering how Steve Bloomer had managed to walk in such clumsy boots. He reminded himself that he had done all he was told to do. He was wearing the right clothes. He had arrived at school a lesson before the game. And he was ready to leave. He had done everything. He was prepared to play his first football game for Charlton Kings School.

His team-mates were already in the corridor, easily recognised by their shirts. They were taller, older and bigger. He knew the school-leaving age was fourteen. He guessed they were all two or three years older than him, some maybe more. Again he felt out of place. He looked for guidance from the teacher in charge of the team. When the man arrived, ready to act as team manager, the young boy concentrated on every word. It was his first team-talk, his first set of instructions, words that could lead him into a football career.

"Here's a penny each," said the teacher, scrambling in his pocket. "You know the bus to Whaddon Rec. I'll see you down there."

The teacher took out his bicycle clips and walked towards the bicycle shed.

The youngest boy felt momentarily deserted. Then he ran awkwardly after his team-mates, not wanting to be left behind. He still felt uncomfortable, physically and psychologically, but sensed his place in the school would never be the same again. He would no longer feel embarrassment about his shirt of many colours. Only pride. He was part of a team recognised for sporting prowess, uniformed and united, all with the same purpose. The belonging had begun. It would last forever.

"Come on, Yarley," shouted a teacher from beyond the touch-line. "Come on, Yarley."

The Charlton Kings outside-left felt a draught as the words brushed past his ear. He chased the ball towards the St Lukes goal-line and jostled with his opponent. Two right-footed players, limited in their options, they tussled artlessly, and the ball ran over the goal-line.

"Corner," appealed the voice from the touch-line.

The boys said nothing. They waited, obediently, for another teacher to run from the halfway-line and make the decision. He said it was a corner-kick.

The two school teams, Charlton Kings and St Lukes, fiercest of rivals, took their positions for the corner, and strange positions they were. St Luke's defenders, all except the goalkeeper, lined up on the edge of the penalty area, 18 yards from the goal they protected. "You can't go past us," one said to a Charlton Kings boy. "You'll be offside."

"Is that right, Sir?" a Charlton Kings boy asked the referee.

The referee didn't know.

"We'll have to ask our teacher at half-time," said another player.

The Charlton Kings outside-left put the ball to rest in the corner of the Recreation Ground. He looked up and his heart sank at the distance he had to kick the ball. He *had* to take the kick; there was an unwritten football rule that wingers took corner-kicks. He decided on his best right-foot toe punt, and aimed for the 18-yard space between the goal-posts and the phalanx of players on the edge of the penalty area. The ball soared across. The boys moved in, some more courageous than others, no one wanting to head the ball. Some turned their backs.

Tim Ward, the youngest on the pitch, was at outside-right. He was ignorant of the professional code which suggested wingers stayed within arm's reach of touch-line spectators. He had only a naive, rustic feel for the laws of the game, a sense that football must have evolved from a competitive need to move an object from one end of a field to another, goals scored by squeezing the object through a designated, measured space, past one player who had special privileges like handling the ball. Tim understood that a pitch needed boundaries because he hated boys who took the ball off to the next field. But it was a simple game really. All you did was chase and kick.

Tim chased the ball into the penalty area and watched the direction of the richochets. The ball dropped kindly into his path from the top of a St Luke's player's head. Tim kicked it towards goal. It went between the goalkeeper and a goal-post and disappeared across the recreation ground. At first he was stunned, uncertain what he had done. Had he been goal-hanging? Had he broken a rule? The boys all looked to the teacher who was acting as referee.

"A goal to Charlton Kings," the teacher said.

A St Luke's boy set off to collect the ball. A group of Charlton Kings boys ran towards Tim. Older and bigger than him, they were intimidating, but Tim knew, from the expressions on their faces, that he had pleased them.

1930

One autumn evening, before dark, Tim went for a purposeful walk, unusually alone. That day he had been selected to play for Cheltenham Schoolboys for the first time. He should have been elated, especially as he was so young, still not yet a teenager, but something worried him. The teachers said he had to bring his birth certificate – to prove to the opposition he was under fourteen.

He walked for a mile, then crossed the road from the allotments and into Croft Road, still wondering what to do when he reached his destination. He had recently learned more about his real mother. He had heard that she had married a man well-known in local sporting circles, a farmworker who lived in a tied cottage. Tim now knew which cottage. It made sense, to the 12-year-old, to visit them and ask for his birth certificate.

He was confused about which was his real family. Did he belong to the Andrews or the unknown tied cottage he was planning to visit? He wondered if the Andrews would have adopted him had he been a girl, because they were committed to boys. A girl would have meant a separate bedroom, whereas the two bedrooms at the Briars could hold five or six boys – the three Andrews boys and occasional nephews.

He reached Cirencester Road and turned right and left before walking down a gentle hill towards a sheltered spot on the edge of farmland. On the left was a row of tied cottages. Tim stood and looked at them, far enough away not to be seen. He gazed for a few minutes, until the detail of the cottages, the stone window-ledges and dark doorways, drifted into a blur. He knew which house he wanted. All he had to do was knock on the door and ask a stranger for his birth certificate, a stranger who was his real mother, a woman he had never consciously met. He walked further down the lane so he wouldn't be noticed loitering. He thought some more. The whole outing seemed stupid to him. How could he knock on the door and ask for a birth certificate from someone he didn't know? He walked up and down. He had no idea what he would say if someone answered the door. He hoped no one was in the house.

Who was this woman anyway? The woman he was visiting. How should he think of her? Was she his birth mother? Real mother? Blood mother? Biological mother? The big worry, always at the back of Tim's mind, was that his real mother would come back for him. She might have had a bad time and wanted someone like him. He didn't know. He wondered what he was doing there.

His aimless walking grew more desperate. He knew he wanted to play football for the town's schoolboy representative team. He knew he had been told to bring his birth certificate. Yet he could not bring himself to walk to the door of the farm labourer's home. He was frightened that they might not let him return to the Andrews family or to the Briars. And when he thought about it some more, he realised how happy he was at the Briars. They had given him a massive canopy bed all to himself, a bed so big that he needed to take a run and high jump at it. And he knew he was treated well by the Andrews family, sometimes even favoured. There was the time he swung a cricket bat recklessly and it slipped from his hands and disappeared through a nearby window. The expected punishment, a spell in boxing-gloves, did not materialise and Tim was surprised.

As he balanced his dilemma – the security of the Briars and the need for a birth certificate – he saw his solution. It was obvious. He would not play. He was happy to sacrifice the chance to play for Cheltenham Boys. He would not knock on the door of the farm labourer's house. He would go home to the Briars. So, less frightened, he walked away, retracing his steps out of the lane, back across to Charlton Kings, back to London Road. He walked quickly and then broke into a trot, finally a run, and for once in his youth wished he could ride a bicycle. He knew he wouldn't mention his walk to Mrs Andrews, the woman he called mother; he knew she would have been furious.

The next day he told his teachers that he didn't have a birth certificate. They let him play anyway. So, to repay them, he played as well as he could, he worked as hard as he could, he ran and ran, and people on touch-lines noticed the lightweight, small Cheltenham outside-right, who chased the ball out of position, wanted the ball, jinked past bigger boys when he had the ball and kicked as hard as the others.

1931

"Come on, young lad," said the Charlton Kings captain. "You're taking this."

Tim stepped up without a second thought. He put the ball on a spot of sawdust 12 yards from goal and players stood out of his way, everyone except the Sherbourne goalkeeper. Tim ran to the ball and struck it sweetly with his right foot. The ball went to the goalkeeper's right, where Tim had aimed, and passed the goal-line. It rustled the front of the net and slithered to the floor. Seven-one to Charlton Kings.

On the bus, on the way home from Sherbourne, while mud was still dropping to the bottom of the bucket of hot water that had served the two teams, the other Charlton Kings players couldn't believe that Tim was still at school. It wasn't that he looked too big and well-built to be a schoolboy; in fact he was very slim and wiry, though he had grown to average height. No, it was because of the way he conducted himself on the pitch. It was obviously that he had practised.

"I've been playing for Andoversford since I was twelve," Tim said, very cautiously. For over a year he had been scared that his school might discover that he was going with his brothers and a neighbouring family to play for a village team three miles east of Charlton Kings. Andoversford officials, respecting Tim's fears, did their best to conceal his name from the list that appeared in the local newspaper. They used a pseudonym. It wasn't a standard pseudonym, like A N Other, or a positional pseudonym, like A G Oaley, A W Inger or Stopall the goalkeeper. It was

J.Ward. "They won't know it's you," said the Andoversford secretary, confidently, but Tim wasn't convinced.

Now that he had been called up to a higher class of football, with Charlton Kings, Tim was not overawed. He was used to changing in pubs, noticing one or two of his older team-mates were missing and being told that they would be "along in a minute" (and smelling of beer). For Andoversford, Tim had played on rough pitches and the goals had had no nets. Rarely did a player score from an angle against Andoversford goalkeeper Picky Leach. He would collect the ball swiftly, slap it down for a goal-kick and put on his best innocent expression. This trick worked more than once.

1932

"Hey, Ward," said Harry Pocket, a driver from Prestbury. "Tell your dad there's a pint waiting for him in the pub."

Tim had been working for almost a year at Lindner's Appliance Works, makers of corn-bins, cabinets and food safes. He was supposedly serving a carpentry apprenticeship but in reality earned his weekly twelve shillings by doing everything except carpentry. It was better than his first job – picking daisies on General Burton's land for five shillings a week.

"I'll tell him that," said Tim. He knew Harry Pocket was his father's friend, and he was familiar with men's banter. He also knew that his father liked a drink or two, either on his way home if his shift at Cheltenham railway station suited, or after waking from a snooze about nine o'clock.

Tim continued loading corn-bins. In the background some of the other lads played with rats, putting long sticks into the bins, waiting for the rats to run to the top of the sticks and then crashing them across the factory with cricket bats.

"How are we doing, young Ward?" asked Harry Pocket.

"There's some more over here, Tim," said one of the other boys.

There was a moment's confusion. Harry Pocket's face grew more lined. "I thought your name was Ward," he said.

"It is," said Tim.

"But he called you Tim?"

"Yes. My name's Tim Ward."

The driver looked more puzzled. "Oh, I'm sorry. I've been calling you by the wrong first name...but I thought you were one of the Andrews family."

"I am," said Tim, but he carried his embarrassment uneasily. He was glad when Harry Pocket pushed his questions no further and drove towards the railway station with a lorry-load of corn-bins.

Tim wondered what would be said in the pub that night. He pictured his father sitting with his drink, an aging man, approaching fifty, beginning to crinkle and wrinkle, sporting a moustache, his trousers held up by braces. Would his father tell Harry Pocket his merchant-navy stories about working as a cabin-boy (until he had second thoughts when chased by a Russian cook wielding a carving-knife)? Or would his father tell of his day's work as a shunter? Or would he explain about who Tim's parents really were? Or did he know who Tim's father was anyway?

1938

They met in the King's Hall, a favourite Saturday night haunt for Derby County footballers and for young women who loved dancing. They talked briefly, but he was reserved. It was odd really. He was a stranger in town, too shy to meet people, yet he was better known than most of the town's inhabitants. He spoke softly, diffidently, in his native Gloucestershire accent, and had to repeat much of what he said. She thought he sounded posh.

She took him on to the dance-floor. She knew he was a footballer – he'd been introduced to her as one – but on the dance-floor she wasn't sure. He didn't know where to put his feet. She helped him round, showed him where to go. She was used to that. Dancing was her passion. As a child she had weaved in and out of dance-room pillars at Taft's.

She was serving a glove-making apprenticeship in an outhouse in Drewery Lane. She told him that. A man called Horace cut out the gloves from skins and showed her how to sew them. She talked about the various designs: bandsmen's gloves with soft leather on the palms and blanco on the cuffs; judges' gloves made of chamois leather and pearl buttons; and the more easy-to-make mittens for kiddies.

She wore a new dress that Saturday night. She had made it herself during the afternoon, treadling and pedalling at her machine after Lily had cut out the pattern for her. She had a new hairdo too. Gertie had washed and set her hair that morning. Gertie knew all about footballers.

They danced and talked, she more confident than him. He knew that his strengths lay in running, kicking and walking, rather than dancing. She earned her living by her hands, he by his feet. She held his hand. He walked her home. They agreed to see each other again.

Nancy Elliott grew up in Derby's "West End". Despite its high-falutin name – by London standards – the West End was short of bathrooms and indoor toilets, and some inhabitants relied on yard pumps for water. Tim wasn't put off by this but he dreaded his first visit to Nancy's Monk Street home. When he was invited for tea, he knew something would go wrong.

Nancy told him about her life in Derby. Her schooling had finished at fourteen, predictable enough for a daughter of a railway-wagon repairer and home-grafting mother. Her first job was ironing fancy clothes in a Duffield laundry. After that she was accepted by Longdon's, a well-known factory a short walk away on Agard Street. Nancy set to work making long stockings, carefully following the instructions on a pattern. Fine elastic was threaded across cone-shaped wheels and then, under the correct tension, taking special care when she reached the complicated ankle design, she would fashion a flat stocking and pass it to another worker for the parts to be joined together. "You've done well to get in there," her mother said when she heard Nancy was earning 15 shillings a week. It was, as they say in the stocking trade, a leg up.

Tim suspected that mothers of young girls did not look favourably on footballers. Maybe they thought footballers were womanisers, or travelled too much, or broke legs and wrenched knees, or drank and smoked and swore and cursed. Tim was more bashful than most footballers. He really didn't look forward to his first visit to Nancy's Monk Street home. Meeting Nancy's family was not his idea of fun. He was sure something would go amiss.

Nancy knew a bit about football of course. He was reassured by that. You couldn't grow up in Derby and avoid conversations about the game. Her Uncle Harry collected photographs from the *Topical Times*. Her brother George might have played for Derby Boys but for an attack of nephritis. Instead George had become a Derby County fan who hero-worshipped left-winger Dally Duncan. "He can turn on a sixpence," George would say, not once but a hundred times, "He can turn on a sixpence."

Tim expected to meet George at Nancy's house, expected George to talk about Dally Duncan, expected something to go wrong.

Nancy's mother laid on a good table. She brought out the best crockery and, specially for the occasion, a new white lace tablecloth. Tim did his best to fit in with the family.

"Can I do anything to help?" he asked.

"You can write addresses on these two parcels," said Nancy's mother. "Ready for the post."

The parcels were handed to Tim, who sat at his tea-table setting and took out his fountain-pen. He remembered that his pen had dried up earlier in the day, when he had used it to sign autographs outside the football ground, so he pulled out the pen's lever to extract a glimmer of ink from inside the rubber tubing. He got more than that. Ink spurted out, straight across the new lace tablecloth.

There was a tense silence.

"Never mind," said Nancy.

Tim couldn't have felt worse had he missed a penalty at the Baseball Ground.

They courted in dance-halls and cinemas. When spring came, they took walks in Derbyshire countryside that reminded Tim of his roots. Nancy was accustomed to breaking out towards rural settings, although, unlike Tim, she used a bicycle. In May, Tim was compelled to return to Cheltenham, where he played a lot of cricket and practised some basic golf strokes across the Gloucestershire fields. Sammy Crooks had found him some golf-clubs.

While he walked the fields, he toyed anxiously with the idea of asking Nancy to visit him there. He asked permission from the Andrews family. They agreed, Nancy agreed, and a forthcoming visit became a big event. But Tim had a problem. Should he tell Nancy about his origins? Wouldn't she find it odd that he had a different surname from his brothers? Should he tell her he knew nothing of his father and very little of his mother? He decided to tell Nancy that he was adopted. He was surprised by her reaction. She was unbothered. A friend of her brother had been brought up by an aunt. Nancy felt she understood.

So Nancy visited Cheltenham for a weekend and, while Tim played cricket among men who wore off-white cricket flannels, black belts and ordinary caps, Nancy talked to Mrs Moss the scorer and then joined the men for the ten-minute walk for tea or drinks in the next village. The Andoversford cricket pavilion was nothing more than a hut, and most players arrived already changed. Nancy grew to enjoy their company, walking along country roads free from cars, watching wildlife stalk the fields, listening to rambling country stories of Gloucestershire people, told in soft harmonic voices.

Tim knew that Nancy was watching him that 1938-39 season. Every home game he had left a stand ticket with the doorman on the players' entrance and she sat alone among thousands of people. She had been to the Baseball Ground before she met Tim, had watched distant figures flit, ant-like, across the grass, weaving patterns that were easily discerned from the tall Osmaston Stand behind the goal.

Tim knew Nancy did not understand the finer details of the sport. She was there to watch her man perform in front of a crowd. She could notice his agility, subtle shrugs of his body and the way he manoeuvred the ball when it was at his feet. Nancy had always thought people clever if they did clever things with their hands, like making dresses or gloves. Now she began to think men clever if they created things with their feet. Tim could certainly do that. There were appreciative rumbles from the crowd if he did something clever. She grew to recognise it herself. Soon she began noticing the other players too and recognised that she was watching a successful team. It was a special season. Tim and Nancy courted, and Derby County courted the League Championship.

1939

Derby County ended that season, a season which had promised so much, in sixth place in Division One. All that remained was the club's dinner-dance at the Midland Hotel.

Near the end of the meal, Sammy Crooks eventually caught on to George Jobey's attempts at eye contact. Sammy had been briefed on what to say.

"I think at this time," started Sammy, "I'd like to hear our esteemed manager speak."

Jobey stood up, looked over the gathering of players, wives and girlfriends. He spoke his rehearsed words: "When I look around at this bevy of beauty, I've come to the conclusion that my players know who to choose for a wife."

Jobey spoke for a few minutes, then called on the youngest first-team player to say a few words.

"I'm going," Tim said to Nancy. He went through the door as if chasing a fast winger.

They drank in the Angler's Arms, a bunch of depressed footballers. Even Tim drank. They knew they were of conscription age. They knew Germany would not withdraw from Poland before the next morning. They knew they had played their last Football League match for a while.

They helped each other into taxis. Went home. Heard the sirens.

Tim sat on the steps of Nancy's home in Monk Street and talked to her brother.

"If they're going to come over here every night we'll have to get a catapult each," one of them said.

Tim walked through the fog to Cheltenham's Lansdown railway station. He had just played for Cheltenham Town against Kidderminster. It was his fifth game for the Robins in the seven weeks after the declaration of war. Expenses were deducted from gate receipts and the players shared what was left. But nothing was left.

After a game, he travelled to Derby to see Nancy. He regularly caught the 5.15 train. Tonight he assumed it would be delayed because fog enveloped the railway station. Had it been dark, the station would also have been blacked out and signs covered. Either way, information was scarce. Through the fog Tim could just about detect the shape of a train. He approached a railway official.

"Is that the 5.15 to Derby?" Tim asked.

"No, no. The 5.15 will be very late. You might have noticed the fog."

Tim settled down to the boredom of waiting. Since the declaration of war, his life had involved a lot of waiting, mostly waiting to join the army. He had gone with other young Derby footballers to enlist at the Assembly Rooms but was deferred for a few months because of a skin rash he had picked up in training. Nothing serious, only a sweat-rash, but it meant he couldn't take a war-work job in case he was later captured by the enemy and in a position to betray military secrets. Instead, having to move out of Mrs Smith's house, he went back to Cheltenham, where his brother Wilf helped him find a job with a furniture-removals firm. The job paid 50 shillings a week, a big drop from an £8 weekly wage. He was not poor – he had some savings – but his life was not in the same division.

Tim watched the train pull out. He was left on his own in the station. He approached the railway official again.

"Can you tell me how late the 5.15 train to Derby is?"

"Oh, it's really late. Hours late. You can tell how late it is – that was the 3.15 to Derby that's just pulled out."

In October Tim's new employer, Barnby Bendall, had a big job in the Midlands. It was 10 days' work moving furniture from Nottingham to Leicester. Tim saw Nancy every day. She was now working at Moore & Eady, machining the band on the top of servicemen's underwear. War work on a piece-rate.

A few weeks ago a First Division footballer had courted a girl who looked after a glove-making business. Now, a removals man and an underwear-factory girl agreed to get married.

1940

The Saturday of the wedding was one of the worst for weather in world history. The conditions caused havoc and hardship throughout Europe: Rome had a very rare snowfall, Berlin was gripped by its worst winter for years and steamers were stuck in the ice of the narrow Oresund straits.

After the declaration of war, the Derby players had immediately lost their contracts and workplace. The Ordnance Corps occupied the Baseball Ground, and a subset of Derby players had re-grouped at Notts County, 15 miles away and on a decent bus route. Notts County had a regular fixture-list and paid players the standard 30 shillings a game. Tim was one of their regular guest players, but not on Saturday 20 January 1940. It was on that day that a boy from Cheltenham's East

End married a girl from Derby's West End at St Luke's Church, Derby. The snow was deep, milk and water froze and people shivered. Nancy's dress and the homemade bridesmaid dresses blended with the climatic backcloth – white on white. At one point in the preparations, Nancy would have settled for a cream suit, arguing with her mother that a bridal dress was a waste of money, but her mother told her to do it properly: "You're the first one to get married. You're having white." As Nancy was still under twenty-one and needed parental permission to marry, she obeyed her mother, and ordered a white wedding-dress from Janette's in Friar Gate.

Nancy's mother and grandmother did the catering, in a reception hall in Nunn Street. The only flaw in the spread was caused by Uncle Charlie taking off his hat and putting it on the food table. Half a packet of confetti floated from the top of the hat and landed in the trifle.

"You daft bugger," somebody said.

The bad weather helped in one way. Tim's Notts County team-mates arrived early at the reception. The local Forest-County derby game had been postponed. No game at Nottingham, but a match at Derby. Otherwise, the weather was detrimental to the occasion. One of Nancy's bridesmaids, her future sister-in-law Della, borrowed a cardigan to keep warm at the reception. Nancy came out of the reception hall carrying her bouquet of Arum lilies, large trumpet-like flowers which she had chosen because high-society ladies carried them. As soon as the flowers hit the frost head-on, they crumpled limply and turned brown.

"We ought to have covered them, Nancy," said her mother. "What a shame. Oh, well, we can't bring them back now."

Nancy knew she would never take uncovered flowers into the open air again.

The next day Tim and Nancy travelled to Broadway in Worcestershire where they could stay with Tim's brother Bill and his wife Alice, both of whom had been at the wedding and had faced a horrendous journey home through the snow. They arrived to find milk frozen in bottles on the doorstep, the cream reaching out above the neck of the bottle. Snow covered everything. It was excruciatingly cold, too cold for football, too cold for anything, but families have ways of providing warmth.

7.
When Life Seemed as Fragile as a One-Goal Lead

On page 32 of my first book, *Football is My Life*, I drew a picture of a green lorry and a small boy in green. The caption was succinct: "On Friday John Tratmann was runn over. His Daddy was a goalkeeper."

It was like losing one of the family.

The Hungarian counter-revolution was in October 1956, about the time Barnsley beat Liverpool four-one. I was largely oblivious to the twelve days of violent street-fighting, and concerned only with the safety of Hungarian international Ferenc Puskas, who was wrongly reported dead at first. I presumed that right-left differences were Puskasian rather than political. Puskas's right foot was for standing on, his left the best shooting mechanism in the world.

We were playing football in our driveway. I tackled my father clumsily and tumbled to the floor. My knee was quite badly cut.

He took me inside the house, washed the cut and stuck on an Elastoplast. Then he gave me a two-shilling piece.

"That's for not crying," he said.

It was my first bonus.

I knew from that, and other events, that he tried to shrug off injuries and illness. A cold was something too trivial to mention. Something he had been through must have given him that perspective.

"What did you do in the war, Daddy?"

"I was away fighting Germans," he replied.

"Did you kill any?"

"Did I tell you about the time I spent a night in a ditch with a German officer?"

Eight Manchester United players died as a result of the Munich Air Disaster. Three of them – Tommy Taylor, David Pegg and Mark Jones – came from the Barnsley region. Local people were visibly affected by the funerals.

Three of the dead players – Billy Whelan, Geoff Bent and Pegg – had played for United Reserves at Oakwell in a six-five thriller less than five weeks before. I had seen that game. It was one of the best games imaginable, and I had spent a long time telling my father what he had missed by accompanying the first team. I had strong images of Whelan, Bent and Pegg: alive, active and athletic.

Three officials and eight journalists also died at Munich. My father talked as much about them: Frank Swift, the former England goalkeeper, who had entertained people like my father with impersonations of a small boy eating hot fish and chips; Eric Thompson of the *Daily Mail*, who deliberately called managers by the wrong name just in case he forgot a name one day (my father was always "Joe Mercer"); Henry Rose, who wrote in the *Daily Express*, the newspaper that was delivered to our house; and George Follows of the *Daily Herald*, who appeared on photographs in my father's scrapbook, taking penalties at Oakwell.

My father didn't think football reporting could withstand their loss. I wasn't sure he could.

A boy at our school contracted poliomyelitis and died.

So did Jeff Hall, the Birmingham City and England full-back.

All the children at our school were inoculated.

So were the staff at Barnsley Football Club.

I was ten when I met Manchester United manager Matt Busby.

"Matt, meet my son," said my father. "He's got a good Scottish name – Andrew."

"Pleased to meet you," said Matt Busby. "And how old are you, son?"

"Twelve," I said. "Er, no, ten."

I was overawed. Not much more than a year had passed since Matt Busby had been seriously injured at Munich.

When Manchester United Reserves visited Oakwell again, I dashed from the stand at the end of the game, sneaked through the players' entrance and stood as close to the top of the players' tunnel as I could. I wanted to be as close as possible to Kenny Morgans when he came off the pitch. He, too, had survived the Munich disaster.

"Who was the Reading player who broke his leg, Dad?" I asked sheepishly. I had not heard the player's name when it was announced over the tannoy as a team change from the programme. I had sat with my fountain-pen poised and nothing to write.

"Willie Gardiner," he said.

His voice was almost reprimanding. I should have known. I'd seen Willie Gardiner play for Leicester City, so I should have recognised him. Late team-changes usually brought in an unknown, but Gardiner had played for Scotland-B.

The next day we went to visit Willie Gardiner in Beckett Hospital.

"If anybody asks, tell them you're twelve," my father said as he led me down the corridors, two or three football books under his arm to give to the patient. "You're supposed to be at least twelve to visit patients."

I was still only ten.

He talked to the injured player. I looked at the immobile leg, and thought of Derek Dooley, whose story was well-known in South Yorkshire. It was only a few years since Dooley had broken his leg playing for Sheffield Wednesday against Preston North End, and doctors were forced to amputate.

This injured player spoke with a Scottish accent. I was always surprised to discover that players never spoke as I expected them to. My father seemed familiar with Willie Gardiner's accent, whereas I could hardly understand a word.

As I write this, I have on the table a brown Soldier's Service and Pay Book. The handwritten letters on the front cover – "WARD, TV" – are barely decipherable after all these years. Inside are his raw details: Army number (7379352 – he never forgot it), surname (Ward), Christian names (Timothy Victor), trade on enlistment (professional footballer), religious denomination (Baptist), enlistment date (16 May 1940 – Leeds), height (5ft 8¼in), weight (148½lb), maximum chest (37½in), complexion (pale), eye colour (brown) and hair colour (black). The pay book is a stark reminder of war.

If the structure of this book I am writing mirrored revelation precisely, this chapter would be near the back. As a child, I heard some of his safe and amusing wartime stories, but the majority remained hidden until I knew what questions to ask. But there was one of his experiences that we never talked about. One day in 1987, as we said goodbye after one of my visits, he handed me a short note which explained what had happened to him in May 1945. I thanked him later. "I thought it would help," he said. It certainly did. It gave me a new insight into his life.

1944

During the war Tim Ward was a Nursing Orderly in the 15th Scottish Division. His unit, the 153 Field Ambulance, was part of the Royal Army Medical Corps (RAMC), and all his training was geared to fitness and emergency treatment. There were parallels with professional football. Run, run, run. Walk, walk, walk. Practice, practice, practice. And, if the manager or commanding officer decided, you would eventually take part.

Early in the 1943-44 season he was moved to a camp near Wetherby in Yorkshire. He travelled to Derby at weekends and played a dozen or so games for Derby County. He played with Raich Carter, and with Leon Leuty, who threw parties and celebrated Tim's homecoming on leave.

An important reason for moving to Yorkshire was to practice river crossings. One such manoeuvre, in mid-February 1944, was Exercise Eagle. It meant 12 days away from camp for most of the 15th Scottish Division but Tim did not take part. He was left in charge of the camp at Wetherby. There were eight men with him, and very little was happening. The other soldiers made inevitable requests: "Let's go home."

Some went home, a couple went to Sheffield for a few days, and Tim was left minding the camp with the help of one other soldier.

The staff-car came on the Thursday. Carrying Major Slater. Bringing trouble.

"We've come to pay your wages," said Major Slater. "Get your men together."

Yes, all two of them.

Tim thought quickly.

"Well, Sir," he said. "I've had a word with them. They don't think it right that we should be paid now and the men on manoeuvres should have to wait for their pay. We're happy to wait for our pay too."

"Oh, very sporting," said the Major. "I'll tell the Colonel."

The Major went away happy. When Tim's colleagues drifted back to Wetherby, they were not so happy.

"That's all very well," said one, "But we're all broke now."

There was only one thing that Tim could do. He sneaked out himself, and played football for Leeds United. Tim earned 30 shillings, plus expenses of 10 shillings (which became a bonus because he had hitch-hiked into Leeds).

Shortly afterwards the manoeuvres were called off, the vehicles too bogged down in the mud. A soldier telephoned Wetherby to warn Tim of the division's return. Tim sent telegrams to AWOL soldiers and order was restored.

"It's obvious we're going somewhere in France," Tim said to Ben Robshaw, the Derby County chairman.

"Is there anything you want, Tim?" the chairman asked.

"Yes, there is actually. We could do with a football."

Ben Robshaw arranged it, and Tim left the Baseball Ground with an extra possession. It was a T-ball, one of the best available. Not a new ball, of course, but capable of surviving a few more kicks. Tim thanked Ben Robshaw, thanked the training staff, tucked the ball under his arm and took the perk back to his unit.

He was ready for war.

Nancy visited him at Wetherby on a rare day off. She was still working hard at Moore & Eady, starting at 7.30, sometimes staying till seven at night. Under poor lighting, in noisy conditions, she worked on the fine detail of underwear manufacture. Her eyes were strained, but the only time she missed work was with German measles. "Not very patriotic," the doctor said.

"I've been talking to Major Slater," she told Tim. "He says you are moving down south. Near Worthing."

Tim knew this meant that action was imminent. They had finished their training and were ready for the game. They would soon know whether the preparations were worthwhile: all those times they had carried 10st of sandbags on stretchers; all that work in the Military Hospital at Thurso; and those freezing troop-ship trips to he would react when he saw his first serious casualty. So much was unknown. Would he come back alive, and, if he did, would he ever play professional football again?

He didn't know where he was taking the old Derby County football.

They were on the south coast at Findon, fully inoculated, waiting to go to Normandy…except, of course, they didn't know they were going to Normandy. It was mid-June, late in the evening, and still light. Tim sat on his bed, next to open French windows, and was disturbed by a strange noise. He had heard about the Germans peppering France with doodlebugs but this was his first experience of one. He looked up and saw the missile, a V-1 flying-bomb, with its strange stubby wings and jet-engine noise, coming over so low that he could have thrown a stone at it. When the noise stopped, the bomb would fall.

An infantry soldier was on guard duty. He fired at the doodlebug with a bren-gun for a long time. He missed persistently.

"You couldn't hit a barn door," said a 15th Scottish soldier.

"Hey, I'm not stupid," replied the infantryman. "If I'd hit it, it would have come down on us."

American-British relations were strained at all levels as the Allies waited for word of embarkation for the Second Front. One night in Worthing, soldiers queued for taxis to take them back to camp after a night out. One taxi-driver drove down the queue until he saw American uniforms. The driver must have heard tales that the Yanks were "oversexed, overpaid and over here". He was looking for an American fare.

Scottish soldiers had heard those tales too. They surrounded the taxi and tipped it sideways. When they came away, Tim saw four wheels reaching for the stars.

The night before they left for Normandy, a group from Tim's unit kicked a football around the beach. An officer walked towards them. He shouted to Tim, his voice serious and officious: "Be careful playing football. You might get injured."

A few days away from violent combat, aware of their physical vulnerability, the soldiers laughed a lot about this. It had, after all, occurred to them that sometime in the near future they might be injured. They were playing football to forget about that.

The vehicles were loaded strategically. All the medical equipment was sealed watertight. Tim saw a space in the lorry, and reckoned there was room for three footballs. His desert-island luxury, the old Derby County T-ball, would be one. He hunted around and found two more footballs that other units in the division were planning to throw away. Three footballs in a space for three footballs. A perfect fit.

Equipped with the reminder of his safety-valve of sport, the outlet from all his problems and battles, he felt ready for whatever lay ahead, frightening though it was.

Tim was lucky with his crossing. It was a golden night, and the sea was flat and of corvettes and cruisers protecting their convoy. "I only hope we can do our job and get back," he thought.

By dawn they could see the church steeples and houses of the French coast. The only sign of activity was the smoke rising from chimneys as fires were lit. The boats arrived offshore and men jumped out and began to paddle for the beach. As they waded through the water, Tim turned to Geoff Bird, a fellow Gloucestershire man. "Well, Geoffrey," he said. "We shall soon be back in Cheltenham."

A few days later, when gale-force winds savaged the water during the worst of the D-Day weather, seasick men rolled off landing craft after gusty crossings. They looked mean and ugly, especially the Scots. At that moment some of them believed that war must be better than seasickness.

The 15th Scottish were chosen by Field Marshal Montgomery for Normandy's first major action. Late to arrive, first to the front. It was an old-fashioned action, a charge deep into the enemy territory to take the Odon River, but well supported by heavy artillery, shells fired dramatically over the heads of the infantrymen at the front.

After four and a half years guarding coasts, they were raring to go and fought with Scottish fervour. When they met fanatical opposition – mainly teenagers from the Hitler Youth Movement – they became fanatical themselves. They fought with everything they had – guns, knives, hands, anger, anything that would serve as a weapon. Some of the hand-to-hand fighting was savage.

The 15th Scottish took La Gaule. They took St Mauvieu. They took Le Haut du Bosc. They took Cheux. But the carnage at Cheux left rubble which slowed the progress of supporting regiments. British tanks came over the hill with bellies momentarily exposed, vulnerable to attack, and were blown to pieces by German guns. The debris added to the traffic-jam at Cheux, while the 15th Scottish pressed on to their objective. Within two days they had taken a bridge over the River Odon, but the Germans fought back and British reinforcements fell behind.

One Saturday morning, Tim sat on the side of a Normandy slit trench with Scotsman Alec Fraser, another of the good friends he had made in army life. Tim was thinking idly about his old and new lives. He knew the fighting had already begun.

The only battles Tim knew intimately were the pseudo-battles of football. They called for team spirit, motivation and the will to win, Perhaps war needed the same. "At least I was used to open-air physical work with other males," he considered. "Unlike some of the others."

He had also worked in a uniform before, albeit the white shirt and black shorts of Derby County. This time, though, instead of a squad of footballers, his team was the 20-odd men of B company, working towards some common goal, following those same principles of football: Let's have no grumbles; Let's get on with the job; Let's do our best.

Dressing-room antics had prepared him well for army banter. Back in Scotland they had got even with an officious RAC lance-corporal by escorting him from Lairg to Golspie Hospital when he complained of tummy trouble. Alec Fraser appeared in front of him wearing a white coat, holding a carving-knife in each hand and muttering something about an operation. "There's nothing wrong with me," said the lance-corporal, which the others had suspected all along. Footballers would have been proud of the prank.

"*Kamarad*," a voice said.

"Was that you, Alec?"

"Eh."

"*Kamarad*."

The voice came again, and Tim's mind returned to his schoolboy comic-reading days. Didn't *kamarad* mean "surrender"? And then he saw them. Two of them. At first he thought they were RAF lads – the uniform was a similar shade of blue.

Alec Fraser spoke first: "Just a minute. If there's any surrendering around here, we're the lads who's doing it."

"*Kamarad*," said the Germans, hands on their heads. They were the first German soldiers Tim had seen. His prisoners.

He was anxious and a little frightened the first time, very frightened the second, terrified the third, petrified thereafter. He learned the old maxim: anyone who says he is not frightened is either a liar or a fool, so when the battle starts, stay clear of him. The 15th Scottish Division helped create the famous Scottish Corridor, seven miles into the German lines but only two miles wide, narrow enough for the Germans to be constantly infiltrating. The threat was always there.

The first soldier Tim treated was a German. He looked at the injured man for a few seconds and then realised he must act quickly or someone might be without a son, someone else without a husband.

He lectured himself sternly: "Come on, you've had four years of training for this. Get on with it."

He simply followed what he had learned in training and applied tourniquets as though the patient was a dummy, taking a blue indelible pencil and marking "T" (for tourniquet) and the time of day on the patient's forehead so the field hospital staff would know how quickly to act. He was surprised to discover that the techniques worked, so he went on applying tourniquets to "dummies"...until he came across a friend. Then he saw them all as human beings.

Suddenly he was surrounded by torn and tattered limbs, pints of blood and psychological effects. Some of Tim's patients couldn't stop shaking. "Bomb happy," it was called, incongruously, and first-aid for "bomb happy" soldiers amounted to two phenobarbitones. Often, what the wounded wanted first was a cigarette. If a patient was in considerable pain a nursing orderly injected morphine and marked "M" (for morphine) on the forehead with the blue pencil.

War might be an exciting, adrenalin-firing place for some people, but Tim soon learned that watching improvised operations was not exciting. And there was always the unsettling noise of shells and the dank smell of battle. The enemy could be anywhere: in woods and coppices, embanked hedgerows, sunken farm lanes, ditches, streams, stone-built barns, farm houses or deep in cornfields. The first few days of fighting took place on ground made heavy through overnight rain.

The nursing orderly's job was to get casualties to field hospital quickly, and in better condition. If he saw a bullet-hole he took a pair of Spencer-Wells scissors, dipped them in a tin and clipped off a piece of gauze which was already impregnated with vasoline and sulphonamide powder. He plugged the bullet-hole, left the scissors clipped on for the moment, and later took them away and applied a shell-dressing. Tim soon realised that a bullet could cause more damage where it came out than where it went in.

He learned to establish relationships quickly: Where does it hurt? Do you want a cigarette? Can I get you a cup of tea? Where are you from? Who do you support? Yes, I can get a message home – just let me have your name.

Some patients were relieved to see him – "Thank God I'm out of it" – but most were in the worst mood of their lives. Sometimes there was no need to ask questions: a soldier sitting quietly holding a blown-off leg; another with half a face; a third holding his head, screaming about his eyes; or a sizzled victim of a tank that had caught fire. Worst of all was immobility. Perhaps a soldier the medical men had grown to know in the last two days.

On manoeuvres in the open country to the south and east of Caen, Tim moved through a cornfield towards a lane at one end. He thought he was alone.

"Psst," spoke a voice.

"Where?"

"Down here in the ditch."

It was a Sergeant-Major from the Black Watch, holed up with a machine-gun for company.

"Nice gun," Tim said.

"Where are you going?"

"Just up to the crossroads here."

"Will you come back this way?"

"Yes."

"When you come back, let us know how many Germans are at the crossroads."

"Oh!"

"Yes, the Germans took that crossroads an hour ago."

Tim stayed where he was.

On the Thursday morning, Tim's unit moved into the cornfield. They were on duty night and day until Saturday afternoon, when a relief section pulled in and started to dig in. A shell fell among them immediately.

"Stretcher-bearers. Stretcher-bearers."

Tim joined in. When the work was over, he counted 18 men. Eight were dead, six wounded and four unscathed. Tim had been there for almost three days, the relief men for five minutes.

"What is it all about?" he wondered.

Tim guessed that one in four of his Division would be killed. More positively, three in four would survive, although he didn't know who. They knew everything about war was risky, but didn't talk about the risks, or about who might get killed. Tim looked around and thought about particular people. *He* could be dead tonight, or *him* or *him*. Tim didn't think it would be him but the fear was always there. His confidence was helped by the knowledge that he was fit, in good condition, and had faith in Montgomery's style. Tim felt that Montgomery wouldn't let them go forward unless there was superiority in numbers.

Next, in Montgomery's plan, came Caen. Operation Epsom. The purpose of the Scottish Corridor tactic was to encircle Caen, an old university town held by the Germans. It was no longer a place for quiet study. The Allied generals planned what in boxing terms would be considered a right and left hook. They took it slowly, feigning that this was the major weight of the forces, giving the Americans, under General Bradley, the chance to move forward elsewhere. By 18 July the Battle of Caen was won and most of the city was at knee-level. Most was dead. Men, women, children, animals, bridges, railways and canals. The place stank with rotting flesh.

Someone had to deal with the dead. British soldiers wore red and green tags. The RAMC took one from a dead body and it went with the dead soldier's belongings, tied up in a green bag, to be returned to Headquarters. At Headquarters they could complete records and compile statistics. At Headquarters they had time, light and safety from immediate attack. Administration was nonsensical on the battlefield.

The RAMC buried dead soldiers in shallow graves, the remaining identification tag still on the body. Later, the War Graves Commission would dig up bodies and complete the task by burying the dead in proper graves. Tim soon learned to make sure dead Germans were buried by live Germans. Just in case the bodies were booby-trapped.

For the first few weeks in Normandy their meals were the same every day: for breakfast a sausage, two hard biscuits and a cup of tea; for lunch half a tin of steak pudding and a cup of tea; and for tea two hard biscuits, a bit of jam and a cup of tea. Then, one day, tremendous cheering was heard from the British soldiers. Tim thought it must be Churchill on a morale-boosting visit, or perhaps a member of the Royal family presenting medals for bravery. No, it was the appearance of white bread. One piece each. Tim took his piece but noticed a small, undernourished French boy standing next to him. The boy gazed at the white bread, saliva forming at his mouth. Tim handed it over without a second thought. The boy went into a nearby cottage and came out carrying a sandwich. He had stuffed the piece of white bread inside two pieces of black bread. Tim assumed the boy had never seen white bread before.

A day or two of rest. At last. Caen taken, they awaited the break-out at Caumont. Tim was too alert to sleep, too wary, too exhausted, too scared.

"Anyone fancy a game?"

He found the Derby County football. Jackets went down as goal-posts. They passed the old T-ball to each other as well as they could wearing army boots. It was the first time Tim had played football abroad.

Estry, France. Early in August. Together with his unit, Tim was in slit trenches from Thursday morning to Sunday evening, and his Division suffered many casualties. On the afternoon of that Bank Holiday Sunday, at around 2.30, one particular German sniper was causing problems from a grove of trees. Some snipers tied themselves in trees to free both hands. Some moved around. Some were hard to see.

It took a while to find someone to deal with the sniper. Half an hour later a tank threw a flame, shots rained on the grove, and the German sniper saw that surrender was the sensible option. He climbed down the tree, brushed himself down, threw off his rifle, discarded his helmet and strutted towards the British soldiers. One tiny Scottish corporal was waiting for him, and everyone except the German knew what was coming. The Scotsman walked to greet the German and, when close enough, nodded his steel helmet sharply. Another casualty. No one seemed too bothered.

The Infantry lost a lot of medical support that day. By the evening Tim's unit was in the front line, advancing with the Infantry into a cluster of Germans with mortars and 88mm guns. Incessant shelling and the inevitable call:

"Stretcher-bearers. Stretcher-bearers."

Tim set off with his equipment. He used his entrenching tool to dig in next to a blazing Bren-gun carrier.

"That's handy," Tim thought. "We can see what we're doing."

He recruited another Bren-gun carrier for the wounded. The carriers were the perfect length to hold a stretcher.

A soldier had lost his leg. Tim put on a tourniquet and, with a colleague, carried the injured man on a stretcher.

Then the blazing carrier was hit again. The blast threw Tim away and made a mess of his steel helmet. He came round slowly. A minute or two went by.

He went with the other injured to the Field Hospital. Tim's wound – a cut on the head where part of his scalp had been taken away – was not serious. What he needed most – like all soldiers – was a night's security and sleep. His two blankets had been fumigated two weeks previously, but had hardly been used since. He rested in hospital for 48 hours and then returned to his unit.

The Germans were in retreat, the British soldiers had sights on Belgium and Holland, and Tim's unit were playing football at the side of the road. A bad pass. The ball ran off the pitch. A tank from the 6th Guards Brigade ran over it. Tim no longer stored three footballs. Only two. Such were the fortunes of war. Such was the punishment for inaccurate passing.

They drove through Normandy. Past smashed vehicles, dead horses, dead German soldiers. The road to Falaise was nauseating. They met the stench of human bodies covered with flies and responded quickly to the strange order that came from their officers: "You may smoke in your wagons."

Tim travelled in the front of a 15-cwt van driven by a member of the Service Corps. The van and a 30-ton lorry could be used as ambulances if necessary.

Tim took a football from the 15-cwt van and a kick-around began. Another bad pass, and the ball rolled under a staff-car which had joined them. "Hey," Tim said. "Pull your car forward. Let us get our ball."

The officer in the car turned round to face Tim, his black tank-commander's beret swivelling through 180 degrees.

"Driver," said Field Marshal Montgomery. "Pull forward a bit."

Tim got the ball very quickly. He assumed the black-bereted figure really was the Field Marshal and not a "double" used on occasion to fool the Germans.

It was the day they crossed the River Seine. A Sunday. Tim was in charge of a section of 10 men – or there should have been ten, it was always less – and they crossed the Seine a mile down river from Joe Redfern's section. Tim learned later that Joe had been hit by a sniper's bullet as he crossed the railway track, his knee smashed and his days as goalkeeper of the unit team probably over.

The wounded were treated. By then it was dark. Six of Tim's section accompanied the injured to the Field Hospital. Tim was left alone. He decided it was unsafe to wander around too much in the dark. He could be shot by either side. Instead he looked for somewhere safe for the night. There were no hedges, only deep ditches with sloping grassy banks. Tim slid into one. After five minutes he realised he was not alone. The breathing moved closer.

"Whose side are you on?" Tim asked, immediately aware of how ridiculous he sounded.

"Not your side," the other replied in perfect English.

"What are you doing here?"

"I came in here to let things pass by."

That made sense to Tim.

The two men soon realised they were both unarmed. The German had discarded his weapons to show his war was over. Tim had been unarmed throughout the war, except for a football.

They talked through the night.

"Where did you learn such good English?" Tim asked. "You must have studied."

"I was at Cologne University. Then I went to the University of Oxford."

Tim explained that the Allied troops were in Brussels, but the German didn't believe him at first.

"And the Romanians have withdrawn from the war," Tim added.

The German officer again looked sceptical. "Where did you hear this," he asked.

"It was on the BBC."

"Oh. If it was the BBC, it must be true."

The Germans were under bombardment. American aeroplanes attacked during the day, British planes at night.

"When the sky's black with planes that's the American airforce," the German said. "When the sky's white with planes that's the British airforce. And when the sky's empty that's the Luftwaffe."

Tim laughed. He hadn't realised Germans could have a sense of humour, and he enjoyed his evening in the ditch. Part of it was like a football game. You fought each other with everything you had, and when it was over, when one team had won, you recognized each other as individuals and teased and laughed and joked. Perhaps you even shook hands and exchanged some equivalent of an international shirt. Or maybe you still hated the opponents for the way they had played and couldn't wait for a whistle to blow and the next battle to start.

The next morning, at first light, Tim led his prisoner out of the ditch and towards the Casualty Collecting Post. When Tim lost his way, the German officer helped. "We go that way," he said, so Tim took him in, following behind.

Three days in action without sleep. When a break came, Tim wanted to play football rather than sleep. Out came the T-ball. There was no shortage of players, and plenty of places to play that reminded Tim of his rural youth.

Jackets went down. Someone went in goal.

"Anybody who scores gets tuppence," the goalkeeper said. "Anybody who misses pays me."

Predictably, the British and the Americans kidded each other about the relative merits of their two air forces. One Sunday morning, at dawn, Allied soldiers stood waiting for hundreds of British bombers to pave the way with a fierce aerial attack. The rain was heavy and the clouds low enough to wash in. Conditions were far from perfect. Yet the RAF pilots brought their planes in at tree-top level and dropped a load of bombs with perfect accuracy and timing.

They were so low that Alec Fraser swore he recognised two lads from his street.

"God Almighty," said an admiring American. "What a thing to do."

"Yeah," said a cool British lad. "But they're 15 seconds late."

On parade. An aircraft hum was heard in the distance.

"That's one of theirs," said one soldier.

Tim was prepared to accept this – he had never learned how to tell a German plane from a British one – but nobody moved. The noise came closer. Everyone stayed on parade. Then the German plane came within range. No one waited for orders. Everyone in the parade-ring scarpered where they could.

Sometimes soldiers hid under hedges, as if they thought they were safe from German planes if they couldn't be seen.

The food improved. With the same rations every day, there had been no need for a cook. Now there was. A few of them tried to cook but their meals weren't popular. A dozen met to decide on the next cook. There was general agreement that one particular lad would make the best cook but he was reluctant to take on the job.

"Alright," he eventually agreed. "I'll do it, but the first complaint and I'm finished."

The soldiers were briefed not to complain. But on the cook's first day, one soldier took a mouthful and shouted an instant reaction.

"Cor, what bloody rubbish," he yelled. Then he remembered the clause in the cook's contract. He looked at the cook and, speaking more softly, he cut through the tension. "But beautifully cooked," he added.

"Corporal Ward," said Major McCallum.

"Yes, Sir."

"Would you organise a football match. We'll be here for a few days. I think maybe England v Scotland."

They had white vests and blue shorts for PT. The other team could play in "skins" or a khaki shirt.

Tim went to find a pitch.

They fixed up goal-posts by driving sticks into the ground.

Football boots were a problem. They couldn't carry them in kit-bags, so they kept a few pairs in the section stores, hidden among the medical supplies because the Staff Sergeant hated football and would throw them out if he found them. The boots were waiting for organised games. A symbol of hope.

A letter from Nancy. She explained that she wanted to buy a house. She had been renting her grandfather's old house in Arnold Street. Now she had a chance to buy it at a reasonable price – £250. It seemed a lot to Tim. But he was earning no money in Europe and had other things on his mind.

At first, Tim was told that his pay was a shilling a day, and he couldn't work out why he was overdrawn after a few weeks. He understood that money was stopped for haircuts, training manuals, barrack-room damage and all kinds, and he knew he was responsible for two pairs of socks, two shirts, battledress, fatigue dress, webbing garters, army boots and other equipment, but he also suspected some fiddle. He was suspicious when he saw dishevelled soldiers return from Dunkirk with virtually nothing to be told they owed money on the lost equipment. One of Tim's unit had abandoned his equipment to save a dozen wounded and later faced a £50 bill. Feelings of injustice intensified when he heard rumours that some people earned £5 or £6 a week on war work in Derby.

Nancy was better off than him. While Tim was unable to draw his full wages and was always in debt, Nancy worked hard and increased her Moore & Eady earnings to £3 a week. She wrote to Tim about furniture, about the house, about the money. She had the money, she was on the spot. He felt poor, estranged, alienated, helpless.

"Who's doing the work in this war?" he wondered.

Having crossed the River Seine, the 15th Scottish Division travelled north-east into Belgium. Always there was routine. Daily they packed their canvas knapsacks, rolled their clothes to fit them in, rolled their two blankets and pulled the straps tight to fasten the knapsack. Day after day after day.

They moved into Holland, and were welcomed warmly. In Tilburg they slept in real beds. They reached Nijmegen and went under cover for five or six days. At Asten, near Venlo, they took over a convent. The nuns had left but had not taken their bedding. The convent was a soldier's luxury.

The soldiers were briefed on what was to come: "Our division will be taking the brunt in here. If we can hold them when they counter-attack the Americans and

Canadians can break around the outside." For weeks they tried to reach airborne troops trapped near Arnhem.

In Best, Tim's company was faced with a German barrage so they dived into a cellar. It was clear they had company in the cellar.

"We'll be lucky to get out without our throats cut," said one soldier.

"You are in quite safe hands," was the reply. "We are the Dutch underground."

Tim grew familiar with the vista on the Dutch side of the Rhine: forests, farmyards and slender factory chimneys which stood like cricket stumps. More like rural Gloucestershire than the sunken *bocage* of Normandy had been. More like, but not the same. But two Gloucestershire men, Geoffrey Bird and Tim Ward, maintained their spirits.

"Cheer up," they told each other. "We'll soon be walking down the Promenade in Cheltenham."

The 15th Scottish also left a trail of destruction through Holland. At Meerhoot they were resisted by two German machine-gunners in a church steeple. A message was sent to headquarters. Headquarters replied: "Give us three minutes." Three minutes later there was no church steeple. It was as though a knife had sliced across its base. The land was flat, the buildings the same.

Tim led the 15th Scottish team on to the field. Local people threw flowers, waved banners and played accordions. A lone Scottish piper played "Scotland the Brave".

Liberation, freedom, celebration.

A football game.

Kit (all black) had been sent forward from divisional headquarters.

Tim met the local Burgomaster at the touch-line and the Tilburg captain in the centre-circle. He was presented with a massive bouquet of flowers and was speechless – he couldn't say "heads" nor "tails". He took the bouquet to the touch-line for someone to hold, and the game started.

For 90 minutes he felt more normal.

After the game he asked for directions to a nearby cenotaph. He walked there and laid the bouquet to rest.

The *Tam O'Shanter* was a two-page stencilled newsletter which arrived daily for soldiers of the 15th Scottish. They read the news aloud.

"Clyde five, Hearts one...Motherwell two, Celtic one...Celtic are 11 points behind Clyde."

"What else does it say?"

"'Queen's Park at Hampden counted up to eight against Albion Rovers. It was a bad day for the Rovers' new goalkeeper, Forsyth of Bedlay, who played for the first time under his own name.'"

The news was greeted with the kind of "oohs" and "aahs" that were audible in thousands at football grounds. The men discussed implications, taunting and teasing supporters of defeated teams.

A Dutch onlooker was surprised at the scene. "You British," he said. "You are the only people who have a war but are more interested in the football."

A Scottish soldier looked up from his newspaper. "Aye," he replied. "And if everyone was like that there'd be *nae* war."

1945

Silence. Even the birds were quiet. Total silence. What he would give now for the 15th Scottish piper, who had crossed the Rhine in a nearby "buffalo" and had sent sound waves into two or more countries. "Silly sod," someone near Tim had said at the time, "Get down the river before they hear you," but the noise of bagpipes was better than this silence. If he did find somewhere to sleep for an hour or two, if he did fall asleep, the silence was so invasive that it would wake him. The noise of shells and smell of battle was unsettling enough, but normal. Silence was the uncertainty. Silence meant battle was coming. Silence was the dressing-room before the game. It was an odd, penetrating silence, lacking background noises that interfere with most silences. Simply silence. A very eerie silence.

The Rhine crossing was over. They waited for an early attack on Germany, waited in silence.

At five o'clock Tim put in ear-plugs to prevent bleeding in the ears. He studied the dawn and waited for the noise of guns behind him. They started firing on Kleve with over a thousand guns and mortars. After two hours of non-stop firing they had a ten-minute break – so planes could bomb the town. They moved into Kleve that afternoon and couldn't find a brick-wall standing. A medium-sized town had been demolished in a morning.

Survivors in Tim's company were now experienced campaigners, combining courage with sensible self-protection. Raw recruits made mistakes. At Donsbreuggen, near Kleve, the Infantry and engineers went on ahead, taking out tele-mines, leaving them on the side of the road. Tim's unit pushed up, past the mines. A sergeant among the engineers, just out from England, went up to a mine and started talking about how to neutralise it. He picked up the mine and started to unscrew the top. Tim's unit ran for cover. They had seen it all before. Months of it. This was March 1945.

Tim was 30 yards away when the mine went off. He survived. Six were killed. The engineer holding the mine was blown to pieces. A man two yards away escaped without a scratch. Ten yards away two were killed. Shrapnel was indiscriminate and unpredictable. It flew up and out, and slit trenches were the safest place to be.

Tim's unit were grateful for digging deep another time in Germany. A Lancaster bomber came down with all its bombs. Two hundred yards away. BANG. It made a hole as big as a field.

Then an RAF plane was shot down. They watched the pilot bail out by parachute, and saw him float down dangerously. Would he land safely or in German hands?

The pilot reached the ground between enemy lines. Wounded in the arm, he walked calmly towards the British side and spotted Tim's medical section.

"Hell of a war out there today, fellahs," he said on arriving.

By the time they reached Holland, the 15th Scottish soccer team consisted mainly of former professionals. One was Joe McCulloch, a skilful, stylish full-back who had played for Celtic. Tim had played with him for the Scottish Army at Ibrox in 1940, had served with him, played with him since. They felt the war might end soon. Then they could play more games together.

Then Joe McCulloch travelled across difficult land in a "kangaroo", a turret-less tank which gave the appearance of hopping. The tank was hit, Joe McCulloch was killed, and Tim was distraught.

In mid-April Tim was given a week's leave. He had been away from Derby for 10 months. A football season had almost passed by without him, but Derby County gave him a game when he came home. Against Doncaster Rovers.

He was a changed man, Derby an altered town, Derby County a different club, although some faces were familiar. Leon Leuty was there to laugh, Sammy Crooks entertained, while Jack Nicholas frightened on the field and Dally Duncan still turned well with a football though not on such a small sixpence.

Tim knew Derby County had been doing well. He had studied the results when abroad. Now he learned that they had what was known in the trade as "a decent team". There was talk of two guest players, well-known players, appearing at inside-forward. Raich Carter and Peter Doherty. They didn't play against Doncaster.

Tim couldn't work it out. He knew he was physically fit and thought his body could withstand anything, but he couldn't play football very well. He wasn't ready for an organised game. Derby lost four-one at home, and Tim learned a new criterion: "match fit".

He wasn't.

He rejoined his unit at Uelzen, Germany, at a camp near the River Elbe. The soldiers sat down for one of the regular writing-home sessions. Someone always shouted out the same advice on how to start a letter:

"Dear mother, is it worth it?"

They wondered. All of them had times when they resented sacrificing so much at such an important time in their lives. Tim still thought of himself as a professional footballer, yet was he really? He had been out at work for almost 14 years, almost half his life, but had known only two seasons when he had drawn a wage for what he did best – playing football.

At best he hoped the war would soon be over. The Germans were in serious trouble now. During an hour's truce to collect the wounded, he was surprised to discover Germans with paper bandages.

Then they were taken to see something beyond their imagination. Ten miles north of Celle. For all Tim had seen, he was unprepared for this. Death, destruction and disease were his constant companions, but not in this way, not like this place. This had everything inhumane in one camp – starvation, disease, physical degradation, slavery, squalor and, above all, cruelty. Thousands of seriously ill inmates lay among thousands of typhus-infected corpses. Deaths were averaging 500 per day and the human bones were knee-deep.

"What is this place?" they wondered in stunned silence, shaking their heads solemnly in disbelief.

The camp was called Bergen-Belsen, or Belsen for short. It was a Concentration Camp.

A warm sun shone down on Belsen the day Tim's company visited, and British tanks came in with flame-throwers to burn the rotting corpses. The Germans had left the camp. There was no one around to arrest, no one for seething Scots to vent their anger on.

Tim's nightmares began that night. He also noticed a change in writing-home sessions. Never again did anyone say, "Is it all worth it?"

There was a silent accord that it was.

Tim had made many good friends in the army, people like Joe Redfern, "Tiny" Seymour, "Lofty" Kerswill, Alec Fraser, Geoffrey Bird, Ernie Hewitt and Jim Temple. One night Alec Fraser reached through the black-out curtain to push open a bedroom window of the house where they were staying in Germany.

The window went out and he fell out with it.

Tim treated him for a broken jaw, broken arm, and broken leg.

He went with him to the hospital.

Two days later. Aronsberg, northern Germany. A day off. The 15th Scottish had worked virtually non-stop for a year. Now they had a whole day to do what they wanted. "Very generous of them," a soldier remarked to Tim.

Tim was hungover from a rare drinking bout. He wanted to fall asleep in the sun. For once football could wait. He sought out a patch of grass and studied the beauty of the weather. Summer, the end of war in Europe and sleep. The world might become a less anxious place. He stretched out in the sun and closed his eyes.

He was disturbed by something banging on his leg. His eyes opened with wartime alertness. Above him stood a German officer with only one leg, hitting Tim's leg with one of his crutches.

"Stand up to a German officer," the man said.

"What!"

"Stand up to a German officer."

As Tim rose to his feet he was aware of what he was going to do. Stirring images formed in his mind. Genocide at Belsen. Joe McCulloch in a burning kangaroo. Dead friends. Six lost football seasons. And sleep disturbed by a German officer who had no right to hit him with a crutch. "There's five years of anger going into this," Tim thought. He was halfway to his feet when he hit the German.

The German keeled over slowly. He fumbled around on the floor, reaching for his crutches, then picked himself up carefully and began to walk away without losing much dignity.

"Where the hell do you think you're going?"

The voice belonged to a sergeant of the Argyll patrol. The German stopped.

"And bloody well turn round and look at me. What do you think you're doing? We've chased you across Europe."

The sergeant and the German officer were face to face now.

"Where do you live?" asked the sergeant.

"Across there."

"That house?"

"Yes."

"You won't in a minute. You'll be in a POW camp."

The sergeant gave the German a hard time for a few minutes, but then let him go. He told Tim that he would have hit the German if Tim hadn't. They exchanged a few matey words, then Tim stretched out in the sun again. He was soon asleep...but dreaming of the concentration camp at Belsen.

Only the T-ball remained. A tank had run over one, and the other had worn thin on makeshift pitches, another casualty of war. Now they played on a beach that overlooked a stretch of water known as Lubecker Bucht. The town was Travermunde, on the Baltic coast, as far forward as the British could be. It was a beautiful holiday-resort setting...were it not for the impact of war. They were not allowed to speak to Germans. There was no fraternisation for six weeks. They kept the football to themselves.

Tim's unit were living in a big house with six or seven bedrooms. In its grounds was a lodge, occupied by a German mother and her boy of eight. The British soldiers warmed to the boy. When field kitchens were set up in the yard, they pushed him into the queue and let him eat. They said they weren't fraternising because they didn't *speak* to the boy. Nor would they reply to the mother when she thanked them effusively: "*Danke schoen, danke schoen.*"

Then another child of the family arrived, an older boy, perhaps 14 years old. His name was Wilhelm. He was indisputably Aryan: upright and proud, with blond hair and blue eyes. When he saw his younger brother queuing with British soldiers Wilhelm smacked him across the face and pulled him out of the queue. This did not endear Wilhelm to the soldiers.

At that time Tim was making daily checks at a nearby hospital. One day he returned to find Wilhelm in the middle of the yard wearing only shorts and shirt. Tim could smell burning.

"What happened?" Tim asked a soldier.

"He came down in his Hitler Youth uniform. We just tore it off and put it in the fire. Look at him. He's still arrogant. Still strutting around as if he owns the world."

After that they ignored the whole family. Other units might have taken more retribution; it was difficult to predict how some soldiers' hatred would erupt. Some would kill anything that moved, anything that resembled the conflict they had been through. Some would kill out of habit. Wilhelm seemed oblivious to the danger he was in.

Five-a-side on the beach. Football at last. The men kicked the Derby County football to each other and began to forget about destruction for a few moments.

When an amphibious craft bounced across the beach, on its way to dumping tele-mines at sea, the footballers shouted to them: "Come across this part, will you? Make sure there's no mines on our pitch."

Tim noticed Wilhelm watching from behind a tree. He walked across to the Hitler Youth fanatic and summoned his limited powers of German vocabulary, knowing that one word was enough to show normality was returning. He planned the word, rehearsed it and said it.

"*Fussball?*" asked Tim.

The small boy's blue eyes suddenly became less stern.

"*Fussball spielen?*" Tim tried.

"*Ja, ja.*"

The boy joined in. He played with them every day.

8. Post-War Euphoria

One Saturday in January, 1956, Barnsley played at Aldershot in the third round of the FA Cup. My mother and I went shopping in the Barnsley town centre. We bought a *Green 'Un* just before we boarded the bus home. We sat downstairs, near the conductor, on a seat that took three and faced the pavement.

A coal-miner jumped on the bus and sat opposite us. He was straight from a shift at the pit. He wore a helmet, his clothes dripped pit-dust and his face was black.

"We won, Mummy," I shouted gleefully after looking at the sports paper. "We won two-one."

My mother was pleased.

"Bobby Brown got them both," I said, excitedly.

I was aware I was speaking loudly and looked up.

The coal-miner smiled at me.

I smiled back.

My mother often cooked rice pudding. She always served me first, gave herself a helping and then passed the dish to my father.

She would encourage him to tell one of her favourite stories.

"Tell Andrew the sago-pudding story, Tim," she said.

And my father would tell us the story. The sago-pudding story was the one I heard most when I was a child. I never tired of it.

"I'll tell you another thing," said my father, conducting an inquest in our living-room after his team had lost that afternoon. "There was a fellow on the pitch today who never got a kick."

"Who was that, Dad?"

"The referee, of course, you silly thing."

I was sitting in my father's office one day and the reception bell went. My father went round the corner to answer it and I heard parts of a conversation with a player.

"But I've been playing well in the reserves at outside-left," the player said. "I thought I was Johnny McCann's deputy. Then when he gets injured you move an inside-forward to the left wing."

I didn't hear my father's reply. He spoke more quietly.

It was something to do with "positional changes", as they tended to be called. People said that my father preferred to make a "positional change" than introduce a new player.

On one of my earliest visits to Oakwell, I gazed at the plush August grass and the players of Barnsley and Notts County as they warmed up for the imminent game. My mother diverted my attention. She was looking at the white-walled alley from where the players had appeared.

"There's Leon Leuty," she said. "He hasn't been well."

She pointed to a man in a suit who stood near the trainer's box.

"Oh, you can see he doesn't look well," she said.

A couple of years after this incident, I sat down with my father to look through his scrapbook, which owed a lot to my mother's endeavours. We came across a photograph of three sturdy men in white shirts and black shorts. They had posed for the camera with arms folded and legs apart.

"That's our half-back-line at Derby County," my father said. "We played together for several seasons after the war. That's me, and the others are Leon Leuty and Chick Musson. The picture was taken at Blackpool."

He paused for a moment.

"To think," he said. "I'm the only one alive now."

It was a confusing picture for me. On the one hand I sensed the insecurity of injuries, migration and possible early death. On the other hand football provided me with a happy, healthy home with jokes and banter. My experience, though, must have been minor compared with my father's. On the one hand there was war, danger and the need to restart his career. On the other hand there was hysterical clowning and post-war euphoria ...with so much still unresolved.

1946

There was a spot of bother at the Midland Hotel on the evening of Christmas Day. Shoes, left outside rooms to be cleaned, were always an easy target for pranksters. One Derby County player threw another's shoes over the balcony, so his were thrown over too, and somehow it escalated. It was a bit rough on the Sunderland players, who were staying in the same hotel. All their shoes went down too.

It was sorted out eventually.

The next morning Stuart McMillan came up to Tim in the hotel.

"You'll be playing outside-left today," the manager said. "Just do your best."

Tim's nervousness was teenage. He remembered that pre-season practice-match at Whaddon Road when he had been picked to play on the wing at the last moment and had then been pulled off the pitch before the match started. Another time, in a friendly against Tranmere Rovers, Tim played on the Cheltenham Town right wing and scored a last-minute goal, his cross from the right touch-line somehow confusing the Tranmere goalkeeper.

Oh, yes, he'd played on the wing before. But not in the First Division.

As an adopted child, though, he had learned to prove himself from day to day, recognising that nothing was ever fully secure. He had been willing to prove himself again after the shock of not being part of a Cup Final winning team.

A boost came with Peter Doherty's arrival at the ground. The players were all amazed that Peter was playing. It had been announced that he had already signed for Huddersfield Town. Now he was at inside-left, playing next to Tim.

Spectators were just as astonished when they saw Peter Doherty. They cheered fanatically when the redhead emerged from the tunnel. The roar hit Tim in the face as he followed Peter Doherty out.

"You should have heard the cheers for me," Tim told his team-mates later. "It must have been because I was playing on the left wing. You ask Peter Doherty. He came out with me."

The hectic Christmas period continued to take shape. The players prepared for yet another hotel meal. A waiter approached Raich Carter.

"What would you like, Mr Carter?" the waiter asked. "Turkey? Chicken? Steak?"

"What I'd really like is some bread, some butter and some jam."

"Excuse me?"

"Yes, I'm fed up of eating brussel sprouts and big meals."

Raich was not alone.

"Bread and jam for the football team," shouted the waiter to the chef.

1947

Alick Grant was the new goalkeeper, signed from Leicester City. At Aston Villa, early in the New Year, a shot from 25 yards flew by him and hit the crossbar.

"Whitewash," shouted Alick, to warn his defenders.

Tim looked across and caught the goalkeeper's eye. Alick Grant made a circle with his thumb and forefinger and held it at eye level.

Everything under control.

Derby County had never played at Bournemouth before. Nor had Tim. He didn't know what to expect. The FA Cup did strange things to players, strange things to pitches. The Bournemouth ground was a sea of water after several days rain. It could have passed for the Baseball Ground.

An odd event happened to him.

He was playing on the left wing again. The pass came from Raich. The pitch was wet, the ball greasy, and Tim made a quick decision to hit the ball first-time down the centre. He felt his right foot slip as he volleyed it with his left. Only then did he hear Raich's call for the ball. "Well, too late, Raich," Tim thought. Raich wasn't pleased, and came out with something ex-dictionary. Tim turned towards Raich, asked if he thought Tim could perform miracles, or something like that.

"What was it anyway?" Raich asked.

"I was trying for Angus down the centre."

When they looked up they saw Jack Stamps talking to them excitedly. Something about a goal. Something to do with Tim.

Eh?

Tim looked into the distance. The Bournemouth goalkeeper was lying on the floor, the ball was in the net, and Tim was told he had scored a goal.

Raich looked across at the scorer. He shook his head and spoke disparagingly: "They shouldn't count goals like that."

A few minutes later the ball came to Tim again. In a similar position. This time he listened to Raich, knocked the ball sideways for him. Raich did a couple of shimmies that only he could do and the ball was in the back of the net. He flashed Tim a supercilious look and spoke authoritatively: "You see, that's the way to score them."

It wasn't until after the game – won two-nil by Derby – that Tim learned how he had scored. His huge kick, from near the touch-line, almost at the halfway-line, had bounced several yards in front of the goalkeeper as he ran out to meet it. The ball had jumped off the wet turf at a surprising height, sailed over the goalkeeper's head and rolled into the net.

"I'm getting fed up of cracking them in," Tim moaned in the dressing-room. He had scored one against Everton in a League game a few days before. "When did you last score?" he asked wing-half Chick Musson.

"Any bugger can score them from the wing," Chick replied in his thick Derbyshire accent.

"But I cracked them in from wing-half."

"When?"

"Er, well, I got one with my first kick for Derby, for the 'A' team."

Chick was not impressed. The two men had a bet. When one scored a goal from wing-half, the other would buy drinks all round after the game.

The bet was settled three years later.

Tim's goal at Charlton, lobbed over Sam Bartram's head, was only marginally better than the freak at Bournemouth.

It cost Chick Musson 45 shillings for a round of drinks, five shillings more than his win bonus.

A few minutes from the end of the fourth-round Cup tie at Chelsea, Derby County trailed two-one. If they lost, it would be Derby County's first Cup defeat for over eight years.

Tim cursed the ball-boys. They moved lazily when the ball went out for a throw-in. Tim knew they were Chelsea supporters.

"Hey, come on, get the ball," he growled at them in his soft voice.

A much louder voice cut through the cold. That of Derby County trainer Dave Willis. The players often teased the trainer about his booming voice, a dozen of them asking him in turn which platform their train went from, creating a one-person chant from the trainer: Platform two, platform two, platform two.

"Get a move on," shouted Dave Willis at the poor ball-boys.

It was an awful day at Chelsea. Spectators shivered. Many had made great sacrifices to reach the ground. The roads were very icy – there had been a lot of crashes – and travel had cost plenty of petrol coupons. The attendance was as low as 49,484.

Then Raich followed up a goalmouth scramble and knocked in a goal with his hip.

Two-two.

Tim was relieved. Now he wanted the final whistle. Now he was happy if the ball was out of play. The Chelsea ball-boys hurried instead.

The ball went over the touch-line to Dave Willis. The trainer, still peeved at what had gone before, picked up the ball and kicked it over his head into the crowd.

There was barely time to retrieve it before the whistle sounded, and the players and officials left the pitch.

As they walked off, Lord Alexander, the former First Sea Lord, leaned over from the directors' box and spoke sharply: "Trainer, that was a most unsporting thing to do."

Dave Willis looked up coldly. "Next time you go to sea," the trainer replied, "Drop off your bloody bridge."

The Haven was owned by Mrs Mugglestone. It was a big house near Mappleton, two miles the other side of Ashbourne, and the directors let the players use it as a retreat. The players relaxed, played games and, in the evenings, sometimes walked into Ashbourne to watch a film.

The guest-house had wonderful food. Somehow Mrs Mugglestone's menu had escaped the worst effects of rationing. Elsewhere, British people had restrictions placed on the food they could buy. Salmon was graded one or two, depending on its quality. One day at the Baseball Ground, a spectator had amused the players after a referee called Salmon had given a couple of dubious decisions. "You're not even grade three," the spectator shouted through the silence.

The wintry weather was worsening. On the afternoon of the Chelsea replay there was some doubt whether the players could travel the 15 miles to the Baseball Ground. They were rescued from Mappleton by jeeps. Nothing new to Tim. Just more army vehicles.

Before the game the players warned goalkeeper Alick Grant about the slippery ground.

"Don't forget, Alick," reminded Raich, as he went out. "No double-jump kicking."

Raich Carter knew the possible dangers from Alick Grant's clearances. The goalkeeper had a habit of taking two quick steps, a hop, a jump in the air and a kick of the dropping ball.

Stuart McMillan pushed past a couple of players in the passage.

"Don't forget," the manager told the goalkeeper. "No double-jumping."

They had only been playing a couple of minutes when Alick Grant caught a long ball, came out, bounced the ball twice, took two quick steps, a hop, a jump, kicked the ball, slipped, fell on the icy pitch and dislocated his shoulder.

Tim and other defenders gathered around the goalkeeper.

What next?

They all looked towards Frank Broome, who stood out on the left wing. They gave him the goalkeeping jersey.

"Okay," said Frank. Then he turned to Leon. "You get everything in the air and I'll get them down the bottom."

Tommy Lawton was Chelsea's centre-forward. The best centre-forward in Britain.

Frank Broome saved everything.

Late in the game, Tim was a couple of yards behind Tommy Lawton when the centre-forward braced himself for a header six yards from goal. "This is it," Tim thought. "It's there." But Frank Broome dived down, clutched the ball and came up grinning with goal-line whitewash all down his jumper.

"This is an international goalkeeper," Tim thought.

The game went to extra-time. The injured goalkeeper, Alick Grant, playing on the wing, helped make the winning goal for Jack Stamps.

It was fairy-tale stuff.

A few weeks later, Tim stood on an orange-box in a Sunderland house and told everyone present about his wonderful FA Cup goal against Bournemouth. The orange-box was the way things were done in the Hunt family.

Raich encouraged Tim to tell the story. He was encouraging Tim a lot. He had coerced Tim into talking at functions, and given him the confidence that his opinions were worth something and that people would listen. Tim might otherwise have been too shy. In return Tim listened closely to what Raich had to say. Such as when they were on a panel together at Heanor, answering questions from an audience. The man from Derbyshire tennis had spoken with rather a lot of "awfullys" for Raich. Raich had replied directly, deliberately accentuating his Wearside brogue: "My contention is that the main difference between amateurs and professionals is that professionals pay tax on their earnings."

Tim shared a room with Raich on away-trips, and Leon Leuty would point to a hotel door marked "WC" and say that it must be Ward and Carter's room. Tim admired Raich, on and off the pitch, listened to him, tried to fathom him. He teased the grey-haired star as "me Dad", as the other players did, and they clowned around with practical jokes, but on Saturdays Tim collected Raich's serious determination. Tim found Raich excellent company when the team won, but sometimes surly after defeat. There weren't too many defeats in his career. He was usually good company.

The grey-haired man talked openly, emotionally, sensitively, and Tim learned about the game, learned about Raich. He learned that Raich had had to fight hard early in his career, at a time when thousands were out of work, paying for his sisters' weddings after his father's death, acting as a surrogate father. So Raich felt that everyone should start from the bottom and work their way up. Tim recognised that what he and Raich had in common was the determination to show that they were as good as everybody else. Raich was brazen about it. Tim kept it to himself.

"Well, I could have given the ball to Raich," began Tim, standing on the orange-box, doing his best to entertain. They had lost at Middlesbrough, but Raich had taken Tim and Nancy to his friends in the north-east for a long weekend. "But I thought that would be a waste of time. I might as well have put it in the stand. So I was considering playing a long ball when, out of the corner of my eye, I saw the goalkeeper move just a fraction. I picked out a greasy patch just outside the penalty area and, knowing it was the start of the game and the maker's name on the ball would be extra shiny, I played the ball with just enough top-spin and the lace the right way up. The goalkeeper was just off-balance enough for it to go over his head."

The Cup run was over now, ended by Liverpool in the fifth round, but Tim felt part of the team again. He was back at right-half, where he could supply passes and watch Raich's number-eight shirt wobble as the English international shifted direction near opponents' goals.

A Thursday morning training session. Very ordinary, except for persistent laughter from Howard Edwards and Jimmy McGill.

"What are you two laughing about?" the other players asked.

"We'll tell you in the bath."

"Come on, stop laughing, get on with it," the trainer shouted.

But the two players couldn't stop laughing. They giggled through training, all the way back to the dressing-room.

"Come on, then, tell us," the other players said, when they reached the dressing-room.

Howard Edwards and Jimmy McGill tried to straighten their faces.

"Give us a few minutes," one of them said.

"Hurry up and tell us, or we'll get the hose-pipe for you."

All the players stripped off their training-gear and stepped in the bath. They all anticipated something odd from Edwards and McGill. They knew them both by now. Jimmy McGill was an extrovert Scot, Howard Edwards a dead-pan man from Stourbridge. For a long time the other players didn't realise that these two were in Bert Mozley's class as practical jokers. They had the ability to play a trick and then stand around sympathising – "That's terrible, who could do something like that?" – but eventually their cover was blown. If they went missing, other players would scamper off to their rooms to check that everything was okay. Chick Musson once returned to his hotel room at night to find all the furniture missing. The room was full of live chickens instead.

"Come on, tell us this story."

So, while the players soaped themselves, washed their hair and provided the usual heckling, Jimmy McGill and Howard Edwards told the sago-pudding story. It went something like this:

The previous day they had rushed home at lunchtime after training. They planned to eat lunch quickly at their digs and get back to the Ground in time to watch the "A" team game, but their landlady, who always went to a lot of trouble, served them lunch in the front room. They did their best not to offend her.

After the first course, the landlady brought in two steaming hot platefuls of sago pudding, or, to be precise, ground-rice pudding.

"I hope you like sago," she said.

"Oh, yes, very much," the footballers replied.

When she had left the room, the players turned to each other.

"Do you want mine?" one of them asked. "I can't eat this."

"No, I don't like sago pudding," said the other.

They found a newspaper and tipped the pudding into that. As the landlady came back, the newspaper was quickly hidden under the table.

"Ooooh, you have polished that off quick," she said. "You must have really enjoyed it. I'll get you the dish."

She came back with the dish, which contained more sago pudding. They spooned the pudding from the dish into the newspaper parcel. By then it was time to go to the match. They collected their gear and one of them tucked the big parcel of sago under his coat.

"Thanks for the meal," they shouted as they left the house.

Now all they had to do was to dump the parcel. Fortunately, a coal lorry was parked forty yards from the Baseball Ground, and the coalman was delivering to the houses in Cambridge Street. The player carrying the parcel bent down to tie his shoe-lace and, with a quick flick of his foot, sent the parcel under the coal-lorry. They went in to see the match.

Afterwards, they mingled with the other supporters as they came out of the ground. One supporter was dressed to the nines. He walked down Cambridge Street wearing a new navy-blue suit. No coat, just his smart suit. And like many people coming out of a football ground, he wanted to play. Supporters could always do better than the centre-forward they've just seen.

When the man in the navy-suit saw a ball of newspaper lying in the road, he took a few quick steps and lashed out with his left foot.

Jimmy McGill and Howard Edwards, following closely behind, had never seen a kick like it. Suddenly there was sago pudding all over the man. All over his suit. Dribbling down his eyebrows. Up his trouser-legs. All over his mates. Everywhere.

When the professional footballers reached the corner, they could see a crowd of men mopping up sago pudding with handkerchiefs. They kept straight faces until they were out of sight. Then they had hysterics. And they hadn't stopped laughing since.

They played at Portsmouth on the last day of May. The season had been extended because bad weather had caused so many postponements. Derby County were in the middle of the League table, and some of the older players from the Cup-winning team had now been replaced; Sammy Crooks and Jack Nicholas had retired, and Peter Doherty and Dally Duncan had been transferred. Tim was one of a succession of left wingers. Another was Kenny Powell, a vegetarian who was usually marked by two colleagues (waiting at the dinner-table for unwanted meat).

Yet another left-winger was Harry McCormick, signed from Coleraine. Tim was present when one of the tactless trainers took a first sight of McCormick. "Bloody hell," the trainer said, "You'd better take him down and weigh him."

McCormick played at Portsmouth on a sun-beaten, solid pitch which suited him. The temperature was around eighty, a complete contrast from January Cup-tie experiences. Ten out of ten experts predicted a home win for Portsmouth. They looked correct when Pompey scored in the second minute, but two goals – one in each half – turned the game Derby's way.

After the game the players were desperate for a drink, but couldn't get one in their Southsea hotel. They walked across to the Pier Hotel, where they saw, waiting for them on the bar, twelve pints of bitter.

"They're yours," the barman told them.

"Ours?"

"The sailor lads bought them for you."

The barman nodded across at the sailors.

"We're all from Derby," a sailor said. "We took bets on you. We won quite a bit."

Tim held up his glass, toasted them, took a sip. It was the first time he had tasted beer in his life.

Nancy spoke with Gil Dickenson, the Derby County director she knew best. The accountant was considered to be eccentric. He wore odd shoes, tipped cigarette ash down his clothes and, over the course of a day, formed an unstable pyramid of discarded cigarettes in his ashtray.

"I was wondering, Mr Dickenson," Nancy said. "Would it be possible to have a club house?"

"But you've got your own house, Mrs Ward."

"I know. But we'd like a bathroom."

The problem with outside toilets was that they were liable to freeze during winter, and 1946-47 had been a particularly cold winter.

"I don't know, Mrs Ward."

But Gil Dickenson looked into it and soon answered.

"There's one coming empty at Sunnyhill," the director said.

The usual arrangement was for the club to own a house and a player to rent it for 25 shillings a week. This one was rented by the club. Tim and Nancy sub-let it. Fifty-seven Sunnyhill Avenue. Tim and Nancy liked it. Semi-detached. So private. There was no stair carpet, of course, and no chance of buying any, but the house had a bathroom. Tim and Nancy sold the Arnold-street house for £750 and moved.

After the Derby County players had played one of their regular summer cricket matches, Tim invited his team-mates back to the house.

"I'm pleased you've come back," Tim told them. "There's a lot of weeds in the garden."

The footballers went into the garden and weeded in the dark.

The new season, 1947-48, brought the usual optimism. A number of First Division clubs knew they were going to win the League, and Derby County were one of them. In Billy Steel, signed for a record fee, they had a new world-class inside-forward to pair with Raich Carter. Stuart McMillan had asked Tim's opinion about Steel. "A good player," said Tim, who had played with Steel in the army. "But he doesn't fit in easily with other players. He keeps himself to himself." It didn't stop the signing.

The outside-left position was still uncertain. For the first match of the season – Huddersfield at home – Jimmy McGill was out of position on the left wing. Normally he played at inside-forward.

During the first half the other players offered Jimmy McGill all the advice they could.

"Out on the touch-line, Jimmy."

"Come back more for the ball, Jimmy."

"Down the wing, Jimmy."

"Get in the game, Jimmy."

At half-time they sat in the dressing-room and tried to sort it out for themselves, as they usually did.

"Jimmy, if you come back a bit I can give you the ball."

"Jimmy, if you go up your wing I can give you it in your stride."

"Jimmy, when you've got the ball…"

Raich had a go at him. Tim had a go at him. They all had a go at him.

In walked Stuart McMillan, the manager. He walked straight to Jimmy McGill.

"Now then, Jimmy," started Stuart McMillan.

Jimmy McGill pulled off his shirt, threw it down, acted animated and spoke mischievously, like a court jester.

"Bugger the lot of you. You can put it on."

The tension cracked. The dressing-room lit up with laughter. They went out and took the game to Huddersfield. Thrashed them. Nil-nil.

Training beckoned but Raich held an audience of players.

"Did I ever tell you about the time we had a problem with penalties at Sunderland?"

The others were happy to listen.

"Our manager was wee Johnny Cochrane. He'd come to us from St Mirren and he always wore a bowler-hat. What a character he was. We came in at half-time in one particular match and we'd missed a penalty in the first half. And we'd missed a few that season, so Johnny started to tell us how we ought to tackle the job. We knew he hadn't played much football himself, and one or two of the lads started to rib him. 'You must have taken a few penalties, Boss. How would you have taken it?'

"'Oh aye,' said wee Johnny.

"'Can you show us what we should be doing?'

"'Oh aye.'

"So wee Johnny took off his bowler hat and placed it on an imaginary penalty spot in the centre of the dressing-room.

"'Stand back,' one of the players said. 'Give him room. Everyone out of the penalty area.'

"He took a few paces back and we went quiet as if our bonuses depended on this penalty. Up he came and he kicked the bowler-hat high in the air. The hat sailed through the air and thwacked against the wall. There was uproar amongst the players. We all cheered and mobbed him.

"'Great shot, Boss.'

"'Great goal.'

"But wee Johnny picked up his hat and turned round with a disappointed look on his face.

"'Well, actually,' he said. 'I hit the bar.'"

Raich's story-telling was interrupted by the voice of assistant trainer Jack Poole: "Come on. Where've you been? You should be out training."

"I was just telling them to get out there, Jack," Raich said.

Tim laughed and went out in a good mood. He loved listening to Raich's stories.

It was Thursday – the day for six-a-side football. Bert Mozley had hung back again. He was last out. This time he had put white in his hair and came out walking like Raich Carter. Bert broke into a trot and ran like Raich. He collected a ball and made exaggerated Raich-like movements with his hips and arms.

The others could hardly kick a ball for laughing.

After training the Derby players and officials ate lunch at the ground. There must have been thirty of them, sitting six to a table. The manager's wife helped serve the food.

"The salad-cream's a bit difficult to get out," said one player. "Give it a hard bang on the bottom."

So someone did.

Bang, bang, bang.

Salad-cream everywhere.

Salad-cream mixed with vinegar actually.

Lunch-times were ideal for pranks.

His ambitions had the quality of persistence. Ambitions continually rise to the surface of the mind. Strong ones stay there. If a thought didn't linger, it was not an ambition but merely a dream, a fantasy or a flight of fancy. Achieving football ambition was hard. Players compromised, and set more sensible goals, or they worked harder for longer. Winning the League Championship took more than eight months' work. Winning the FA Cup meant winning six matches over a period of four months. But who knows how long it took to win an international cap? Was it a whole career? Several years? A successful season? Or did it take only a few minutes of deliberation from a selection committee as the administrators voted for who should occupy each position. To the recipient of good fortune, success could be sudden.

Stuart McMillan walked towards him in the dressing-room. The manager, as usual, was dressed superbly. He stood over him and spoke with a slight smile.

"I've some good news for you, Tim. The England selectors have chosen you for the game against Belgium."

Sudden success. It was all he could ask for. He was picked for England. He had proved himself to his family. He had come all the way from his origins, if he really knew what they were.

But what if they didn't want him at the last minute?

What if he was injured in the meantime?

What if the game was called off?

"Believe it when it happens," he told himself. In the army he had learned to live from day to day.

In the dressing-room at Wolverhampton, Tim had a visitor. It was his first Derby

County manager, George Jobey, who had left the club in 1941, suspended after an investigation into illegal payments.

"I always knew you'd get in the England team," said George Jobey. "You were one of the best players to play under me."

Tim smiled. This was rare praise. "You've never said that to me before," he said.

"Ah, well, you're in the England team now."

Tim met the England players at the Great Western Hotel, next to Paddington station. They saw the Football Association treasurer individually.

"Ah, you're Ward, aren't you?" said the treasurer, when it came to Tim's turn. "Let me see. There's your train fare from Derby to London, and the same again back."

He didn't need Tim to tell him the pounds, shillings and pence. He had it in front of him.

"And there's your bus fare across London."

Tim looked at the elderly gentleman who was telling him his expenses, and had to restrain a laugh. Memories of tales came flooding back: of big Frank Swift telling stories about trying to claim his expenses; of Tommy Lawton talking about the time the treasurer, short of change, had to overpay him by a penny but made sure he sought out Tommy at the next international – "Ah, Lawton, you owe us a penny, don't you?"

Only now did Tim realise that the stories were true. They really did calculate expenses to the halfpenny. After collecting his expenses from the treasurer, Tim realised that there was no allowance for a meal on his return journey from London to Derby.

They travelled by boat to Belgium. It was a historic occasion. A group of journalists gathered to form the Football Writers' Association. They suggested an annual award – Footballer of the Year. Stanley Matthews was a likely contender.

Saturday's training included some fiddling with the ball. Then they were broken down into small groups.

"Have a word with Stan Matthews and Stan Mortensen," said England team manager Walter Winterbottom. "Tell them how you're going to take throw-ins."

Me? Tell them? Tim kept his thoughts to himself. He had lost most of his shyness now, but telling the two Stans seemed beyond him.

They played the international on the Sunday. Heavy tropical rain softened the ground and drenched many of the 75,000 spectators at the Heysel Stadium. In the first minute Tim found the ball at his feet, playing for England. He pushed the ball to Stan Matthews. Stan gave it him back. Tim pushed it forward to Tommy Lawton.

"This is good," Tim thought. "I'm going to enjoy this."

He got the ball again, passed to Stan Matthews and waited for the return.

The return never came.

Instead, Stan Matthews set off on his own, shuffling the ball from foot to foot, zigging and zagging, dropping one shoulder, then the other, either fooling defenders about where he was going next or simply being too quick with the motion. A feint to go inside, a switch to the outside, a short, sharp sprint and he was away, dodging players like he was weaving through a crowded Blackpool beach during Glasgow week.

"Is he going to pass to me," Tim wondered. "Yes, he is. No, he's not."

In the opening 20 minutes of the game, Matthews laid on three goals. He had never played better for England.

It was wonderful to watch, but something worried Tim: What should I be doing while Stan Matthews threads his way past players?

At half-time Tim had a quiet word with Wilf Mannion, England's inside-left.

"What should I be doing, Wilfie?"

"Just keep giving the ball to Stan."

"What should I do if he doesn't give it me back?"

"Come and queue up on the penalty spot with the rest of us."

Belgium two, England five.

In the dressing-room Tim noticed that Stan's boots were worn down in the same way as his own. He had always been a little embarrassed by the strange wear-and-tear. Now he would parade it proudly.

On the morning of a match at Charlton, Howard Edwards, the Derby County reserve, came down for breakfast and told the other Derby players about his dream.

"We conceded an early goal," said Howard seriously. "But we played well after that. We went on to win five-one."

"Who got the goals, Howard?"

"I'm not sure. I didn't have a very good seat in my dream. There must have been a pillar in the way."

That afternoon two mid-table teams took the field for their 18th League game of the season. When Tim walked in the dressing-room after the game he saw a wry smile on Howard's face and immediately recalled the dream. Yes, Charlton had scored first, just like Howard Edwards had said. Yes, Derby County had won five-one, just like Howard had dreamt.

"Great dream, Howard," someone said in the bath.

"We'll have you as reserve every week if we play like that."

"We'll ask the Boss."

They were very superstitious.

"Any dreams last night, Howard?"

"No, not one." replied Howard Edwards, now the team's regular reserve. "I stayed awake all night trying to have a dream."

Had he told the players they would lose seven-four at Preston, they might not have believed him. But that's what happened. An incredible game. Four-four with 17 minutes to play. Three late goals to Preston North End.

Stuart McMillan, the Derby County manager, went round everyone in turn. He asked them what had gone wrong.

"This fellow Tommy Finney," said goalkeeper Billy Townsend.

"This fellow Tommy Finney," said right-back Bert Mozley.

"This fellow Tommy Finney," said left-back Jack Howe.

"This fellow Tommy Finney," said right-half Tim Ward.

The manager soon got the message.

One Wednesday afternoon Tim sat in "B" Stand with a group of first-team players. They were watching a Reserve team game.

Johnny Poppitt was playing full-back for Derby County Reserves, defending on the far side of the pitch. The terraces alongside him were empty, their turnstiles kept shut for this game. Johnny Poppitt made a tackle, overbalanced and fell over the boundary wall. There were no spectators to break his fall. He disappeared from sight and everybody speculated on how he might have landed.

"He could be badly hurt," said a first-team player in "B" Stand.

The players on the pitch ran over to the touch-line. Their concern was obvious, even from a distance. A couple of them leaned over the wall to see the damage to Johnny Poppitt. Someone motioned to the trainers.

"It must be a stretcher-case," said someone near Tim.

The players on the pitch looked baffled and bemused. They patently did not know what to do. They called for more help.

The lads in "B" Stand saw Johnny Poppitt before the players on the pitch did.

"There he is. Behind the goal."

Johnny Poppitt was grinning widely. He had crouched down, run 30 yards out of sight and kidded them all. No wonder the players on the pitch were baffled. Johnny Poppitt had disappeared.

Tim and the others thought it hilarious. They talked about it all week.

The players' room at the Baseball Ground was crowded with people. It was a happy room, opened recently by the Arsenal captain. There was enough beer for two teams.

Howard Edwards was telling a long story about Steve McLachlan's war adventures. The familiar dry, serious voice had talked about McLachlan's heroic escape from the Germans in the desert, talked about the recapture, and was now explaining the second escape. The tale of the first escape was extraordinary. The story of the second escape was unbelievable, except that it was a story about Steve McLachlan, so everyone believed it.

The captive audience – players and players' wives – held their mouths wider and wider.

"...and then Steve was alone in the desert, not a drop to drink, not a bite to eat," continued Howard Edwards. "He went four days in the desert, nothing to eat, nothing to drink, his mouth as dry as a bone, the sun streaming down, no sign of civilisation, left for dead . . ."

Rather than continue with the story, Howard Edwards walked to the door, as if to leave. Everyone protested.

"What happened?"

"What happened next?"

"Oh, he was lucky," said Howard Edwards. "A Bird's Cake Van came along."

It was a generous club. At Christmas they put on a party for the players' children. They gave each family a bird of their choice – chicken, turkey, capon, anything they wanted.

Tim and Nancy chose goose. It needed plucking. They sat in their kitchen and pulled off feathers. Soon, feathers were everywhere, floating around the kitchen, landing wherever they landed.

One of them coughed. The feathers that had already landed now jumped up again, floated around some more, and again landed wherever they wanted to land.

They plucked feathers for hours.

A neighbour came in.

"It helps if you wet the goose first," said the neighbour.

"Oh, does it?"

The day after Boxing Day. Five up against Blackburn. Bobby Langton had the ball again, out on Blackburn's left wing. Tim knew what to do. It was habit now. They had a way of stopping the England international winger.

Tim moved towards the left winger and forced Langton to turn inside, enticed him to take the ball towards the centre of the pitch. Langton obliged.

Tim knew Chick Musson was waiting. Chick tackled hard, standing up, shoulders sloping, chest sticking out in front. Bobby Langton wasn't tackled by an isolated boot, or even a complete leg, but by twelve stone of Derbyshire brawn. All of Chick Musson.

Chick knocked the ball away. Tim collected it, controlled it, looked for Raich or Billy Steel or Reg Harrison or Jack Stamps or Angus Morrison, and went about his Saturday job.

But Leon Leuty also wanted the ball. Leon was everywhere. Defending and attacking. Up for corners, back for corners. Playing centre-forward, playing centre-half.

"What's up, Lee?" Tim asked him.

"I've got us in the sweep," Leon replied. "Most goals."

A corner at the Derby County end. Billy Townsend, Derby's big, burly goalkeeper, picked himself off the floor to take up his position. He was wearing his cap. It was a big cap with a press-stud and a pull-down front. As the ball was placed for the corner, Leon crept up behind the goalkeeper and pulled the cap down over his eyes. Other Derby defenders laughed too much to mark players.

"I've been dying to do that all season," Leon said.

The corner was cleared, but Bobby Langton had the ball again, coming in from the left wing, facing Tim. "Come on, Bobby," Tim thought. "Let's have you inside again." Tim's mind subconsciously carried Chick's words, spoken with an accent as broad as his shoulders: "Lave 'im to may, lave 'im to may."

As Tim went side-on to Langton, the left winger obligingly took the ball inside, touched the ball past Tim. Then Tim felt two arms around him, hugging him. Langton had stopped in his tracks.

"Oh, no, Tim," said a Lancastrian voice. "Not this time, Tim. Not with Chick waiting again."

1948

He was injured half an hour after the start of a third-round FA Cup game against Chesterfield. He had occasionally thought about injuries but hadn't expected any to happen to him. He had sprained an ankle jumping off a lorry during army training, but his football career had been relatively trouble-free.

He played a simple pass, like thousands he had played before. He stood still afterwards. Where the player came from he had no idea.

A numbness struggled down his back. He reached with his hand to hold the area of his back that had been hammered by the player's knee. Tim cursed himself. He should have known. Why else would Chesterfield have played a defender like him in the forward-line? Why else would he have been charging after Leon and myself?

"Has the referee sent him off?" Tim asked the Derby County trainer.

"No."

Tim hauled himself to his feet, felt the cold water. He continued with the game. Played all the way through. Didn't enjoy it one bit. Only the final whistle. Even then it was painful.

One consolation was the result.

Derby County two, Chesterfield nil.

Two years after Derby County had won the FA Cup, they were at it again. It was the start of another Cup run. They were almost arrogant at Crewe when they played their fourth-round FA Cup tie. Tim was fit again. They were all fit. And playing well. Thirty-one goals in 10 games. What had trainer Jack Poole said before this game? "I'm willing to bet that Crewe won't turn up when they see our team."

A Third Division North team was a Third Division North team, even if they had beaten First Division Sheffield United in the previous round.

The Crewe players turned up. One Crewe player turned up wherever Raich Carter went. Late in the game, when Derby got a left-wing corner-kick, Raich drifted slowly out of the penalty-area pack. He trotted towards the right wing, as far as the corner-flag, over 70 yards from where the corner was being taken. Raich picked the post out of the ground and handed it to his marker from Crewe, who had followed him all the way.

Their wives saw the game. The club had taken them to Crewe for a day. Took them there, brought them back. The players knew Derby County were good like that. A great club, they told each other. All that golf. One laugh after another. Nothing but good results.

Crewe Alexandra nil, Derby County three.

Through to the fifth round.

Derby County footballers stood at the bus stop. Bags of golf clubs rested on the pavement. Wednesday meant a day playing golf. Manager Stuart McMillan was all for it. He was a superb golfer. Tim, Leon and Raich were of a much lower standard, much the same as each other. When Leon was good he was really good. When he was bad he was really bad. Whether he was good or bad, he gave everybody a good time.

They travelled by trolley-bus, even though two or three of them now had cars. Jack Stamps had bought an old banger with a loose passenger seat which caused passengers to topple backwards when the driver put his foot down. Tim hadn't yet thought about driving a car.

As the bus came towards them, Bert Mozley hung back from the crowd. The others knew something funny would happen.

The bus stopped and the players got on. They had no need to pay, especially

Raich. He had little need to carry money around Derby. Now that Peter Doherty had left for Huddersfield Town, and Sammy Crooks had retired, Raich was Derby's superstar. Bus conductors winked at him. He travelled free on trolley-buses.

Bert Mozley, pipe in his mouth, was last on. As he boarded the trolley-bus, he kicked the step, stumbled forward and, as the bus pulled away, writhed around on the floor with only the bowl of his pipe visible in his mouth.

The conductor and other passengers looked aghast.

"He's swallowed his pipe," someone said.

But Bert had unscrewed the bowl of his pipe from the stem.

The other players guffawed. Life was a music-hall joke.

The fifth round of the Cup offered an away tie at Middlesbrough, another First Division team. On the Friday there was an accident in the Baseball Ground gymnasium. Billy Townsend fell down and broke his wrist. He was the club's only professional goalkeeper.

Two hours later they set off for Middlesbrough with a teenager called Frank Payne. He was the only goalkeeper registered to play. He had played a few games in the lower teams.

The young goalkeeper had a bad night, but Jack Howe offered to take all the goal-kicks for him.

Somehow they got through the game.

One time, when the goalkeeper held the ball and looked like being shoulder-charged into the net, Leon, thinking quickly, kicked the ball out of the goalkeeper's hands and on to safety.

Middlesbrough one, Derby County two.

Stuart McMillan went out and signed Jock Wallace of Blackpool. He was one of the few goalkeepers who weren't Cup-tied, but he hadn't played much that season.

"Hey, take it easy," said a Grimsby Town player. "You've got the sixth round next week."

In the past, playing against the Cup favourites, Tim had said similar things himself. Grimsby, bottom of the league, needed points. Derby County, third in the league, lent some thoughts to the Cup.

Tim wasn't sure he wanted Grimsby to go down. Maybe the other lads felt the same. All that free fish was nice twice a season, and it was refreshing to walk along the sea-front from the Lifeboat Hotel.

Billy Steel shot long and low into the Grimsby penalty area. Jack Stamps, back to goal, stood on his right foot and waved his left heel as the ball reached him at knee-height. The ball set off on a crazy loop and somehow drifted into the net.

Jack Stamps carried his surprise uneasily.

The other Derby players looked embarrassed.

They could do no wrong.

"We can't help but win the Cup," Tim thought.

They didn't see a football the week before the sixth-round Cup tie at Queen's Park Rangers.

"Whatever you do, don't touch a ball," said Jack Poole, the trainer. If he said it once he said it a dozen times. "Don't touch a ball. We don't want any more accidents like we had with Billy Townsend."

The club's pranksters saw their chance. They held a meeting on the Thursday. Bert Mozley, one of the club's best actors, was given the part.

On Friday morning they took a light-bulb out of one of the gymnasium lights. They sent a young groundstaff lad out for some tomato ketchup. Someone pinched a box of talcum-powder from the treatment-room.

Bert Mozley lay down in the gloomy corner of the gymnasium. The others rubbed him with talcum powder. He was looking like a ghost when they tipped the ketchup over him.

Raich was the first to leave the gymnasium. Jack Poole was working in the dressing-room when Raich walked past.

"Somebody will get killed in that gymnasium," mumbled Raich. "The way they carry on." He walked through to the bathroom.

"Oh, my God," said Jack Poole. "They're not playing in the gym. Not this morning."

The trainer hared down to the gymnasium as quickly as he could, while Raich slipped into the manager's office to warn Stuart McMillan that everything was alright.

When Jack Poole arrived in the gymnasium, he found Bert Mozley collapsed in a corner, almost dying.

"Don't worry, Jack, I'll play," said Bert Mozley from the far distance. "Get me stitched up and I'll go out and play for you. I'll do my best for you, Jack."

"I suppose you'd better tell the Boss, Jack," someone offered.

The trainer went nearly as white as Bert Mozley looked. It was some minutes before the ruse was revealed.

It was no picnic for a trainer at Queen's Park Rangers. A tough sixth-round Cup-tie was in progress. Billy Steel was injured, limping feebly on the wing. Jack Stamps came off to have his cut stitched. Frank Broome, the reserve, was helping with the stitching when he turned round, started to run and knocked himself out on a concrete beam that ran from the ceiling to the floor.

Not easy for a trainer. A match going on. One on the field who needed nursing. Another in the dressing-room needing stitches. The reserve unconscious on the dressing-room floor.

Queen's Park Rangers one, Derby County one.

Replay next Saturday.

Jack Stamps, head swathed in bandages, scored twice in the replay. So did Raich.

Derby County five, Queen's Park Rangers nil.

Semi-final next. Only a week away.

Confidence was not a problem. Not for a team averaging more than three goals a game over the last 16 games.

Whenever they travelled to London, they saw a show on the Friday night and played the match following day. One time Bert Mozley lost the return half of his ticket.

"It'll be alright," he said. "All the tickets are numbered. We're all in rotation, so I'll be able to work out what number I should have, and it will be obvious that mine's missing."

They all had a drink on the station before catching the train. Bert came out of the station-bar early and explained his plight to the ticket-collector.

The other players reached the barrier.

"Do you know this gentleman?" the ticket-collector asked.

"No, we've never seen him before."

"We get a lot of hangers-on."

"You rotten lot," said Bert Mozley.

But Stuart McMillan, the manager, vouched for Bert.

Tim usually gave his complimentary tickets to Ted Kerney, a keen supporter who lived just round the corner in Stenson Road. Tim liked him, thought him a nice, quiet chap, and gave him two tickets for most of the Cup games that season. The semi-final was no exception.

This time Tim walked round to Ted Kerney's home and put them through the letter-box.

Ted's dog chewed them to pieces.

Ted Kerney spent two days sticking the tickets together with tape. Eventually he completed the jigsaw. On semi-final day, Tim went with Ted to the club office at Sheffield Wednesday's ground. They explained the situation to Eric Taylor, the secretary, who replaced the tickets with two more.

"No one could make up a story like that," said Eric Taylor.

It was very quiet in the Derby dressing-room after the game. Nobody spoke. "It's no good going over those three terrible goals," Tim thought. Especially the third, just when we'd pulled back a goal, just when we were playing well. No good shouting about it. He looked at the other players. They all looked at each other. It was over. Done with. Tim had never worked so hard or concentrated as fiercely as he had in those last fifteen minutes, when 22 players and 60,000 spectators had lived solely for the next kick. He had never felt this bad about a defeat. Even the players who had won at Wembley were affected.

Derby County one, Manchester United three.

They were out of the Cup.

Blackpool – including Stanley Matthews and Stanley Mortensen – would play Manchester United at Wembley.

A fortnight later Raich left for Hull.

Tim knew about football now. You mark a great player in your first game. Then you meet him. Then you play with him. Then he signs for your team. Then you get to know him. Then he moves somewhere else. Then you remember him forever.

After Raich left, Tim shared a room with Leon Leuty on away trips. The end-of-season trip to London took in the Festival of Youth, Footballer of the Year awards and the Cup Final. Leon, Tim and Raich demonstrated football skills on stage for the Festival of Youth. Leon was on tenterhooks. His horse had won the Oaks, and he had backed a horse called *My Love* in the Derby to give him a double. A hundred pounds was a lot of money.

The Guest of Honour at the Festival of Youth was Princess Elizabeth, who was in the public limelight, pregnant for the first time. In her speech she praised the people who took part – like the ballroom dancers and the footballers – and was in full flow when Leon's voice cut through the quiet of the audience.

"It's done it. It's won."

My Love had won the Derby.

The party went back to the hotel and Leon entertained them with his winnings. He stayed in London and said he was going to Ascot for a week, even though it meant missing the Rams cricket game at the Ordnance on the Tuesday.

Come Tuesday, however, the first person Tim saw was Leon Leuty.

"We didn't expect you till next week, Leon. What are you doing here?"

"I'm bloody skint."

"You've lost all that money?"

"I put it all on *Pearl Diver*. They lifted the tape and it turned round and set off in the wrong direction."

Leon laughed at his misfortune and Tim laughed with him. Leon was not one to hold grudges. He never quibbled if he lost. He only made others laugh.

"I don't think I'll back any horses with Pearl in them again," Leon said.

9.
A Little Bit of Success in The League

We used to play guessing games, my father and I, usually over breakfast, when we shared a dialogue stimulated by newspaper articles.

"Who's the new manager of Huddersfield Town?" he asked one morning.

"Eddie Boot," I guessed.

"Right first time. Very good."

It wasn't that hard. My father and I had discussed it already.

Two weeks later I was stumped.

"Who's the new manager of Grimsby Town," he asked.

I reeled off a few guesses.

"Ivor Powell?"

"No."

"Raich Carter?"

"No."

"Sam Weaver?"

"No."

"Nat Lofthouse?"

"No."

I had run out of ideas. We were in the kitchen on a cold February morning and the boiled eggs were nearly ready. I shivered in front of a one-bar electric fire and grew more interested in breakfast. I didn't want to play the silly game any longer, especially when I wasn't winning, so I made a ridiculous guess.

"You," I said.

"Yes," he said.

When I saw he was serious, I went into a mild state of shock. My knees went weak and I almost toppled over the electric fire. Other football managers changed jobs. Not my father. He had been Barnsley manager for almost seven years.

It would be weeks before the reality dawned. I had to say goodbye to friends, change schools, learn a new accent and refer to a different team as "us".

My father went on ahead, my mother stayed in Barnsley to sell our bungalow, and I continued at school in Wakefield. One March day I went to see the headmaster to ask if I could leave school early. Saturday morning school was a problem if I wanted to see a football match. One of my class-mates had told me that he had been allowed to leave school early one Saturday to see his father. I thought I'd try the same approach.

"Er, I'd like to leave thirty minutes early, Sir," I told the headmaster. "Er ... this Saturday morning ... so I can see my father, Sir."

"I'm not sure about that," said the headmaster. "Are you sure you don't want to leave early just to see a football match?"

Maybe he knew that Grimsby Town were playing at Mansfield and that my father wouldn't be available until after the match. The headmaster refused permission.

That Saturday I dashed out of school as soon as we were dismissed. A lift to Mansfield was waiting for me. We sped full throttle to the game and arrived in the directors' box just as the Grimsby players celebrated an eighth-minute goal.

"Cullen," the directors told us. "Mick Cullen."

But I found out later that Jimmy Fell had scored the goal.

I studied my new heroes and grew to recognise them, but the game went Mansfield's way. They led three-two when Grimsby tried a last attack. Our full-back headed from long range, the ball travelled in an arc towards the Mansfield goal, a fist went up and punched the ball over the crossbar. I knew it wasn't the goalkeeper's fist but no one around me noticed anything. The referee gave a corner-kick, and I began to doubt myself.

"I thought someone handled at the end," I greeted my father.

"We should have had a penalty," he said.

So I was right after all.

The first game I saw at Grimsby was settled by a peculiar goal. Reading full-back Ray Reeves took a free-kick from the halfway-line. The ball floated high into the biting east-coast wind, and Grimsby goalkeeper Alan Barnett moved out and then stepped back. He did a few stop-start sprints as he would in a training session. Five yards forward, three back, three forward, five back.

The ball went over his head, into the net.

Reading were near the bottom of our division, Division Three, and I wondered if moving to Grimsby was the right thing.

It was an odd experience, I suppose, supporting a football team as the manager's son. Very few kids have their father's job scrutinised so often by so many. As he was working at small clubs, he was the only football manager in town and I was the only football manager's son.

His work was very public. It was difficult to avoid being known as "Tim Ward's son". Perhaps that's why my parents considered leaving me at Queen Elizabeth Grammar School, Wakefield, as a boarder. In the end, we agreed that I would move with them. We packed all our belongings in tea-chests and moved to Grimsby. When we arrived we couldn't find a kettle.

There was always a story to be told. Did you hear about the football manager who changed jobs and hired a removals-firm to shift his possessions? At the end of a long, arduous day, the removals men sat on tea-chests in the kitchen of the manager's new house, and drank tea and chatted idly.

"Are you the new manager?" asked one of the workmen.

"Yup."

"Should we leave our lorry round the corner…so it's handy?"

My father negotiated with the headmaster of Clee Grammar School. It took some time because I was still only 10 years old. I spent a week in limbo, kicking a football against the garage wall of our new bungalow, inventing one-person games, such as left-foot against right-foot. I was much encouraged by our proximity to the sea. If Stanley Matthews really did perfect his body-swerve on a crowded Blackpool beach in the summer, as my father said he did, then Cleethorpes was my chance for stardom.

I started school a week into the summer term.

A few days later two new class-mates approached me. They had made the connection.

"Are you any relation to the new Town manager?"

I owned up proudly.

I had my first friends.

My father showed me his new office. We walked through the Grimsby Town board room (shaped like a ship's cabin) and into a very small room heated by an electric fire.

On the white door was black lettering: "Manager's office".

It was his first private office.

"This is where all the work's done," he told me. He said that to everyone he showed in.

We went outside again, and walked across to the secretary's office in a separate building.

"This is Byron Robinson, our secretary," he said. "This is my big lad, Byron."

At Grimsby, over the next two seasons, at a crucial time of my development, I learned that football could be very rewarding, so I shall dwell on the success. Take our start to the 1960-61 season. We were unbeaten for the first seven Division Three games, and the eighth was a floodlight game at Bradford City. I was eager to know the result but my bedtime curfew was before the news came through. The next morning I asked my father.

"Oh, Bradford City won," he said. His face wore a tired, gloomy look.

"Bradford City won…Grimsby Town three."

His face now showed the smile of another Grimsby Town victory. He took delight in my change of expression.

It was just his bit of fun.

Barnsley came to the east coast just before Christmas, 1960. They were the enemy now. I wanted them to lose.

We beat them three-two.

Ron Rafferty headed three goals and I loved him for it.

I had a new hero. Ron Rafferty could jump higher than a crossbar, higher than a goalkeeper's outstretched arms. He could head goals from 20 yards, and shoot with either foot. There was nothing he wouldn't do for me.

Living on the east coast, my mother and I worried about the extra travelling that the team had to do. Sea-frets submerged the coast, and returning from away games was sometimes an ordeal. In December 1960 we read that the Sheffield Wednesday team coach had crashed coming back from London. A 19-year-old reserve inside-forward called Doug McMillan had had his right leg amputated just below the knee. My father said McMillan was at the front of the coach only to change the radio station.

"Be careful, Tim," my mother said.

"Come home safely, Dad," I said. "But come back with some points."

During the summer, I would occasionally spend a day-out among the amusement arcades of Wonderland. Syd and Joe owned Wonderland. They were my father's favourite Grimsby Town directors. He talked about them occasionally. Joe, he said, was generous and noisy. Syd, he said, was generous and quiet. Syd never said much in board meetings, but what he said was usually to the point. Two hours of one board meeting was spent discussing why a director's wife didn't get a half-time cup of tea. The board decided to buy a second tea-pot.

"That's the important business out of the way," commented Syd. "Is there anything trivial? Like whether the manager wants any players?"

Another director stressed that they should be prepared to travel anywhere to sign players.

"I saw a useful lad last year in Monte Carlo," said Syd. "I fancy going back."

Two hours of another board meeting was spent discussing floodlights. The existing lights were no longer suitable. Someone mentioned that Wolves had sold their floodlights to Blackpool, but Blackpool might not be able to use them. The matter was deferred.

The next day my father took a phone call from Syd in Blackpool.

"I've bought the floodlights," the director said. "Could you make sure there's someone at the ground when they arrive."

My father spoke of this incident with gratitude. He wanted me to know the difference between saying and doing. He knew Syd didn't want people to know, but he told me, and now I've told you.

In 1961-62, the season I reached my teens, Grimsby Town achieved some tangible success in the League, thanks almost entirely to my mother and I. Oh, I suppose the players did something too, and I guess my Dad did pick the team, and someone like the trainer must have kept them fit, but it was my mother and I who discovered the horseshoe at Christmas. We hung it over my bed and rubbed it carefully before each game. Two rubs on the left, two on the right.

Thanks to our efforts, Grimsby Town started to win and win and win. From a mid-table position we crept up the table and entered the Third Division promotion race. It was all thanks to my mother and I rubbing the horseshoe. Our roles were sophisticated and subtle, not crude and obvious like those of the players.

We forgot once and lost to Queen's Park Rangers at the White City Stadium. I might not have forgiven myself, but our overall record with the horseshoe was good enough – seventeen wins, two draws and only two defeats.

My school pals pumped me for information. In return they fed me stories from the annals of Grimsby Town's history. They told me about that time when the Dynamo Prague goalkeeper kicked the ball and a following wind carried it to the edge of the Grimsby penalty area, where it bounced and soared over goalkeeper Malcolm White's head for a bizarre goal. I envied them their role as witnesses. That goalkeeper's goal was from a previous era, almost 18 months before we had moved to Grimsby. I was developing a keen sense of history.

Some of my school-mates knew a lot about my father. They knew who should be in his team and who he should sign next. But I knew things they didn't. I knew he put Silvikrin on his hair, used Colgate toothpaste and put pieces of toilet-paper on his face when he cut himself shaving.

Along with my school-mates, I read newspapers and programme pen pictures, but I had unfair access to extra details. I knew that Grimsby Town right winger Johnny Scott could flip up a penny, catch it on his foot and then flick it up into his jacket pocket. I'd heard my father say that inside-forward Mick Cullen touched every piece of wood in the dressing-room before he left for the pitch (last in line). He also told me that Cliff Portwood received interesting dressing-room visitors such as Karl Denver, the top-ten singer. At a reserve-team game, I heard players call Johnny Pearce "Tough" when he took a throw-in, and my father confirmed his nickname, presumably from Alf Tupper, "The Tough of the Track". I learned that centre-forward Ron Rafferty was the team's joker, not beyond setting up a false photography session for a new player, like he did with left-winger Freddie Jones. At the club they called him "Chips" Rafferty.

"Why's he called Chips," I asked my father. "Does he eat chips?"

"There's an actor called Chips Rafferty," my father replied. "An Australian actor."

I tried Johnny Scott's trick with the coin. I tossed up the coin, tried to catch it on my foot and spent five minutes searching for it under the sideboard.

After a school lunch, our stomachs crammed full with boiled vegetables and heavy puddings, we played football. We spread blazers as goal-posts and ran around with ridiculous energy, doing our best to keep grass-stains off the long trousers we had just started wearing. We didn't play "football", we played "togger" with "a pill", and goalkeepers were "one and you're in" or "running-back goalie". We argued when the ball went near a goal-post.

"It was in."

"Post."

"Would have gone in off the post."

"Would have hit the post and come out."

"Would have come out, hit the goalie and gone back in."

Plastic balls were in their infancy, but we learned that heading a plastic ball with an incorrect technique didn't hurt as much as heading a real football properly. A new game, "centres and headers", arrived on the curriculum. One lunchtime I jumped up to head the ball like Ron Rafferty did – with power and a sharp flick of the head. Something clicked in my neck. I couldn't move my head back. This wasn't supposed to happen. The ball should have flown into the corner of the net like it did for "Chips".

I went to the staff-room and saw the games master. He reassured me it was nothing serious and mentioned the name of the muscle. I don't recall the name. Latin was never my strongest subject because it rarely appeared in football reports.

When I got home, my father looked at my neck. He seemed to know about injuries. He took me to the club, and into the medical room, where physiotherapist Jimmy McCoy examined me. Around me, older men told stories of how chief scout Jack Topliss could get into a really hot bath.

"It just needs a bit of heat," said Jimmy McCoy.

I spent a day holding my head over the electric ring of the cooker and thought myself very professional. Later, I realised that the physiotherapist had meant something else.

Everyone wanted my father to sign new players. He had signed Cliff Portwood and Freddie Jones during the previous close-season, and Dennis Fidler more recently, but it wasn't enough. One Saturday in October, he went to Cardiff to scout a player called Peter Donnelly. I stayed home and watched Grimsby Town draw one-one with Queen's Park Rangers. I realised that his first news of the Grimsby match would come from me. I couldn't wait to tell him about Ron Rafferty's goal, and all the rest.

At seven-thirty on Sunday morning I woke up my parents with a cup of tea.

"...and then, Dad, Dennis Fidler shot...and their goalkeeper dropped it...and Ron Rafferty just touched it home."

I borrowed a few more phrases from the *Saturday Telegraph* and talked non-stop: "And we played in blue shorts, because they had red shirts...and their red shirts clashed with our red shorts...and...and..."

I learned much later, when he was in a better mood to tell me, that he had left Grimsby at about 6am on the Saturday morning and had driven his Austin Cambridge as far as Derby. He had continued to Cardiff by train. After the match he had rushed to Cardiff station for a return train and arrived in Derby about 10pm. Five miles out of Derby his car had broken down. A motorist drove him back into Derby, and it took two hours to fix the fault. He arrived home about 6am, exhausted.

He'd been asleep for about an hour when I came in with the tea and told him every known detail about the match he had missed.

When I misbehaved in class one time, a monitor put my name on the blackboard. I was destined for trouble when the teacher came back so I offered a bribe.

"I'll tell you who my father's trying to sign if you take my name down."

"Okay."

"Alan Banks of Liverpool."

The board-rubber swept from side to side.

My father never signed Alan Banks, but it was the truth at the time.

Afterwards I felt guilty.

It was the first time I had betrayed his confidence.

I wouldn't do it again.

That season of success, 1961-62, had some low times too. We were knocked out of the major Cup competitions by poor Fourth Division teams: three-two at Mansfield in the FA Cup, and three-two at Doncaster Rovers in the League Cup. I saw the game at Doncaster, when our team surrendered a two-nil lead. I winced at some of the tackling, and Doncaster's low floodlights were painfully dazzling. It was a long, tiring journey home. My eyes smarted from the persistent glare of car headlights, one set after another, lights after lights after lights. I was tired of lights that night. When were Doncaster going to get some proper floodlights, like our new ones at Blundell Park?

I remember a dismal game against bottom-of-the-table Newport County on a cold and misty day in December, a game marred by an accident to a young Newport inside-forward, Alan Finlay, who collided with our goalkeeper Alan Barnett. Barnett stood up quickly and threw the ball into the crowd. I can still picture the anguish on the face of Bobby Evans, the Newport player-manager, as he stood over the stretcher and watched blankets being pulled over his fellow Scot's broken left leg. Newport played with 10 men for 80 minutes and Grimsby won one-nil. My mind recalled my father's words after news of a two-one defeat for Hartlepools at Exeter City: "A long trip home for them tonight."

Two Grimsby players, Malcolm White and Duncan Welbourne, contracted tuberculosis, which kept them out for several months. Everybody at the football club was tested. Everyone at school was inoculated too.

In December we lost at Watford. My father returned home with an incredible story of how the game had been stopped for 10 minutes so that groundstaff could fill in a two-foot wide hole in the pitch. The hole was as big as a bucket, and the groundsman wheeled a barrowload of soil on to the pitch. Some of the players had to be hurriedly brought back from the dressing-room after the work had been completed. It was the way things were going at the time. A mid-table team looking for a hole to fall down.

One of the few players he signed that season was a Scotsman called Willie Purvis, who knocked on his door because he had moved from Berwick-upon-Tweed to start a job with a Grimsby dock firm. In the New Year, Willie Purvis played six first-team games and scored two goals. His enthusiasm was enough to get the winning run started. His enthusiasm and our horseshoe.

Lacking new players, my father defended the ones already there, and I passed on his words to my school-mates. Mick Cullen got "the bird" from the crowd (whatever "the bird" was) but my father liked him, and that was what mattered. He told me how Mick Cullen "made the team tick", and I told my school-pals. I also told them about Cliff Portwood's initial difficulties settling in Grimsby, and they had no answer to that, especially when, early in the New Year, that wonderful year of 1962, Cliff Portwood juggled the ball daintily and scored miraculous goals. He reminded me of Johnny McCann. And the wingers became more exciting. On the left, Jones the speed; on the right, Scott the skill. All they had to do was put the ball near Ron Rafferty, because all my school-mates liked him. I only wished that my father had signed him.

We were 12th in Division Three at the turn of the year, then won seven in succession. Ron Rafferty scored in every game – 10 goals in seven games. We played at Lincoln on a Friday night, and my father was in a good mood. He laughed a lot about a story he heard that night. He told me the story the next day.

Two Grimsby supporters set off for Lincoln on a motor-cycle. The level-crossing gates at Hibaldstow were closed. The motor-cycle stopped in a queue of traffic, and the pillion passenger got off to stretch his legs. But the motor-cyclist saw a way to weave through the traffic, and the gates conveniently opened as he reached them. He opened the throttle and was at Caenby Corner before he realised that he had no pillion rider. "Oh no," the motor-cyclist thought. "I've lost my passenger." He turned round and spent the evening looking for him. He searched all the roadsides, checked every hospital, missed the match.

At the level-crossing, the pillion rider eventually caught a country-bus back to Brigg and hitchhiked home to Grimsby, although one version of the story suggests that he had got a lift to Lincoln with the next car and watched an exciting one-one draw.

Ron Rafferty scored our goal at Lincoln.

He scored in the next match too.

Grimsby Town three, Northampton two.

He scored two in the first-half against Queen's Park Rangers, one of a number of teams chasing promotion, but something went wrong with our two-nil lead.

Queen's Park Rangers three, Grimsby Town two.

"I mustn't forget to rub the horseshoe again," I told myself.

"Mustn't forget."

"Mustn't forget."

Ron Rafferty scored a brilliant winning goal at Bournemouth, another of our rivals for promotion. The next day my father entertained me with the dramatic story of the last few minutes. The referee allowed five minutes of injury-time with the score at three-two and Bournemouth on the attack.

"Hurry up and blow, Ref," said Ron Rafferty. "I've got a train to catch."

"It's alright," said the referee, Ken Aston of Ilford. "I'm on the same train as you."

"You'll miss your train, Ref," said Rafferty, a minute later.

The last home game of the 1961-62 season was against Watford. My father came home at lunchtime and told me about an incident that would affect the afternoon's game.

Watford were staying at the Lifeboat Hotel. Goalkeeper Dave Underwood turned round, tripped over a team-mate's bag and put his hand through a plate-glass window. A doctor was called for. Underwood was stitched up. It was too late to call up another goalkeeper.

We won five-three.

If we won at Brentford we were promoted.

My mother went down to see that game. I stayed with friends and waited to hear the result.

Brentford nil, Grimsby Town two.

For the next month we inhaled euphoria. My mother couldn't stop talking about the night-out in London and Eartha Kitt's act at the "Talk of the Town".

When the news broke that Ron Rafferty had spent the last two months of the season with a damaged knee cartilage, he was an even bigger hero.

That season, 1961-62, supporting Grimsby Town among friendly people, my football interest was strengthened by the rewards the sport could bring. Or was it? Perhaps my football interest was as strong as it could be before that...or even before I was born. My mother was pregnant with me for most of the 1948-49 season, the most popular football season in

British history. On match-days, she took me to the Baseball Ground, home of Derby County Football Club, where a 30,000 crowd regularly cheered and groaned and rumbled and roared. She took me there because her husband, my father, was a professional footballer, and she enjoyed watching him work. She introduced me to football before I was born.

1948

The first game of the 1948-49 season was at Manchester United. Derby County won two-one. A new player called Cyril Thompson was at centre-forward. He had joined the club from Southend United, and was still finding his way around town.

"Get off here and cut through Arboretum Park, Cyril," someone said, as the team coach approached the Baseball Ground.

So Cyril Thompson stepped off into the dark, walked into the Arboretum and tried to fathom the park's meandering pathways and multitude of exits. The next time he saw the lads he claimed he wasn't home much before breakfast.

Welcome to the team.

Three wins and three draws in the first six games. It was a good way to start a season. Perhaps this was their League Championship year.

Then Sunderland at home. Two down and a penalty to Sunderland. Jackie Strelling took it. The ball stuck between Billy Townsend's legs. Someone scrambled the ball away.

Derby scored twice in the last six minutes and were still unbeaten.

Bert Mozley was injured against Bolton. A pulled muscle. When he wasn't pulling other people's legs, he was pulling his own. He was at risk wherever his body was cold. If a trainer came on the field to treat another player, Bert had to keep exercising.

Bert moved to the forward-line and helped to create a goal for Frank Broome five minutes from the end.

Derby County one, Bolton Wanderers nil.

Unbeaten after 10 League games.

Howard Edwards was reserve at Liverpool. Who else?

Frank Broome had a heavy cold so Howard was told to change. Someone went out to find a doctor who could examine Frank Broome. Howard Edwards stripped for action.

A few minutes before kick-off, a doctor came in and examined Frank Broome, decided he was fit to play.

Howard Edwards watched another game. It was the closest he ever came to playing a League game for Derby County.

It finished nil-nil.

Match number twelve was at home to Preston North End. Jack Howe was on international duty, so Tim captained the team for the first time. He responded to the local anthem – "Now is the Hour" – and led the team down the passage. He turned right, took them to the traditional end for kicking-in.

He called tails. He always would.

They beat Preston one-nil.

They hadn't lost yet.

Unbeaten runs hung on threads. Frank Mitchell took a penalty for Birmingham and missed it. Billy Steel immediately scored at the other end.

Birmingham City nil, Derby County one.

Fifteen League games without defeat.

This was Championship form.

Trouble at a night-club in Liege. Steve McLachlan had two Belgians pinned to the floor as he ranted and raved about the war. Four more Belgians stood by, petrified.

They came no more masculine than McLachlan. He wasn't often a first-team player, but he had always been a first-team man in the army, a front-line fearless Scot. Back in peace he often flared up. One time, in a rage in the dressing-room, he turned out his pockets and four little acorns fell out. They were symbols that he had been mentioned in despatches four times during the war. Everyone could believe it. There was a quiet respect.

"What got Steve het up in the night-club?"

"I think it's just the Belgians. He was in the 51st Highland Division. He thinks they were let down one time by the Belgians. Says they allowed the Germans to sneak through and attack."

Earlier that day Derby County had played a friendly in Liege.

Match day number 16, and Tim caught the bus to the Baseball Ground. There were seats available on the bus. Most spectators were already at the Baseball Ground, their group mind registering the tension, emotional chords waiting to be plucked. The crowd arrived before the players. Tim made a privileged late entrance.

He arrived an hour before kick-off. He was careful about time. He had once had a scare before a reserve-team match immediately after the war, when his bus was caught up in a fog and he arrived only 20 minutes before the Central League team kicked off against Leeds. The trainer was furious. Tim was lucky he wasn't replaced by a reserve.

For the home game with Middlesbrough he made no mistake. He got off the bus at the Cavendish and began the walk to the ground. Streets were full of familiar sights in Derby. A Bird's cake van, a very pale custard colour, with its striking motto: "We never sell a stale cake." Ah, the security of familiar sights. Outside the Baseball Ground there was often a tall, vacant-looking supporter who the players knew as Pigeon Percy because, when he wasn't leaning over players' shoulders watching them sign autographs after training, he simply stared up at the sky.

Plenty of familiar sights, but the walk to the ground felt different without Raich alongside.

"Are we going to win, Tim?" asked a voice from a doorstep, someone not going to the match.

Talking with spectators outside the ground would add a few minutes to his journey. He sifted through the people who pleaded with him to be let in, and looked for those he knew to be genuine supporters. Most players smuggled in one genuine supporter, taking him down the tunnel and on to the terraces before getting changed. Tim never forgot meeting an ex-army acquaintance who had walked 10 miles from Ripley but was shut out at 11 o'clock. He had heard other tales of what people did to watch him. They queued for hours to get tickets for Cup ties, warming themselves in a variety of ways – with coke braziers from a nearby foundry, by playing impromptu football in the street or by taking turns to save a place while one disappeared to the fireside of a nearby house. People stayed overnight to get tickets, wrapped in rugs, drinking from vacuum flasks, blue with cold by morning.

Middlesbrough was the eighth home game. Another crowd of over thirty thousand. Another win for Derby County.

One Sunday Tim and Nancy sat in their living-room listening to next door's wireless. The neighbour was almost deaf. His wireless was on full volume.

Tim heard someone saying his name.

Tim Ward.

"There must be lots of Tim Wards," he thought. "Is it anything to do with football? Maybe I'm reserve for the England team. Isn't that announced today? Or maybe I've misheard."

Ted Kerney was the first to the door. He was breathless. He had run from round the corner.

"Have you heard?" Ted asked. He could see Tim hadn't. "I've just been listening. You're in the England team to play Wales."

A few more neighbours came round, and Tim and Nancy turned on their own wireless. The small crowd laughed through "Take it From Here", and then mimicked the voices of Joy Nichols, Jimmy Edwards and Dick Bentley.

England played Wales at Villa Park, Birmingham, on 10 November 1948. Tim's mother, Eunice Andrews, saw her son play football for the first time. A neighbour drove her to Birmingham. Her husband had died during the war, while Tim was on the boat to Normandy.

Tim was playing right-half for England, but full-back Lol Scott was carried off after 23 minutes. Nobody told Tim to drop in at full-back, but he looked around him at the empty spaces and decided he ought to cover as much ground as he could, especially as Stan Mortensen, the inside-right, was an attacking inside-forward and the other inside-forward, Len Shackleton, was injured too.

They went in at half-time and Tim expected a team talk. He thought someone might make positional changes, perhaps swop him with the other wing-half, Billy Wright, who had more international experience and was captain. But no one said a word about the missing full-back. And Tim did not speak up. He would regret it later. He would resent having to play out of position.

It was touch-and-go whether Len Shackleton came out for the second half but he did. He played on the left wing. Tommy Finney came inside and played like three. Tim knew that if he got the ball he could give it to Stan Matthews or Tommy Finney.

They played with virtually nine men, and it was the first time Tim had played right-back. He was pleased with himself, delighted with the result.

England one, Wales nil.

Derby County players at the match said how well he had played.

The newspapers were full of praise for him.

He received a treasured letter of thanks from Arthur Drewry of the Football Association.

The selectors never picked him again.

The scenes at Newcastle were incredible. The first fans arrived at 4am. Those from nearby talked about "Oor Jackie", meaning England centre-forward Jackie Milburn.

"What about our Jackie?" asked a few Derby County fans.

"Who?"

"Jackie Stamps."

They sat outside the ground and read newspapers ("Son for the Princess Elizabeth").

By midday miners from Northumberland and Durham villages had arrived in their hundreds. Some time later the referee came from Goole and the two linesmen from Teesside. By kick-off it was an incredible sight at St James' Park. The official attendance was 64,061, but Tim was sure there were more inside the ground. Maybe 80,000, maybe more. And they estimated 20,000 were shut outside. Tim did not know numbers. All he knew was what he saw. He saw them fetching kids down over the top of the crowd before the game. He saw them sitting the children on the track. Tim politely stepped through them when he wanted to take a throw-in, then turned his back on thousands who had come to see the game, and threw the ball.

The top two teams in the country, and the sport's biggest season.

Derby started the game leading the First Division by three points.

Newcastle United three, Derby County nil.

Defeat in the 17th League game of Derby County's season.

They were now a point clear.

Number 18 was another big game. Portsmouth at home.

In the 10th minute Jack Froggatt took a hurried swipe at the ball and completely missed his kick.

"Here's you leg back, Mister," shouted a spectator.

Billy Steel scored the goal.

Derby County one, Portsmouth nil.

Derby County were drawn against Southport for the third round of the FA Cup. Southport at home. The Southport chairman, Jack Lord, was a Derby man who always made Derby players welcome when they visited the north-west.

After the Cup draw, Jack Lord sent Derby County a telegram. One of the players read it to the rest.

"Recommend you play the game at Southport."

They had a good laugh about that.

Bert Mozley was injured yet again. He moved to outside-right against

Manchester United. And scored. But it wasn't enough. Derby lost three-one. And at home.

They were third rather than first.

1949

Near the end of the fourth-round Cup tie against Arsenal, which Derby won one-nil, Ian McPherson powered in from the wing to try a shot. Tim reached the ball slightly later, blocked it with his left foot. The ball squirted away harmlessly. Tim went down holding his ankle. He could feel it swelling up as he held it.

He remembered about ankles. Make sure you keep the boot on. If you take the boot off, and the ankle swells up, you might not get the boot back on, and you might not be able to finish the game. He had once criticised the Derby trainer for taking off Leon Leuty's boot at Liverpool. "You shouldn't have done that," he told the trainer. "Don't worry," Leon had replied. "It's my other ankle that's injured."

"It's my left ankle," Tim told the trainer, explicitly.

He didn't know what it meant. Except that he was probably out of the team for a while.

Two months later a coach was driven into Rugby in Warwickshire.

"Crikey," said a fellow called Ryan, the "A" team trainer. "Have you seen the placards?"

Tim looked out the window, read the placards: "England international plays in Rugby."

It had come to this – Rugby Oldfield against Derby County Colts. Anything to get a game. After two months in the wilderness.

It had been a difficult two months. He had watched a few first-team games, growing increasingly frustrated as Steve McLachlan or Bert Mozley took the number-four shirt in his place. He had watched Derby County beat Cardiff in the FA Cup (gates shut 45 minutes before kick-off) and then go out to a late goal at Portsmouth in the sixth round (gates shut 80 minutes before kick-off).

He had tried all sorts of remedies to cure the injured ankle. There was a Birmingham specialist who twisted his ankle in every direction, and Tim couldn't put his foot to the floor afterwards. And another chap in Stoke. What a laugh he was, mainly because Jimmy McGill, the club's extrovert practical-joker, had travelled to Stoke with Tim, and Jimmy McGill knew all the specialist's mannerisms from earlier visits. Tim enjoyed Jimmy's impersonations, but his ankle was no better after the visit.

Now it was time to give it a try. He rubbed plenty of Algipan on the ankle and strapped it up. Then he went out and hobbled through a game against Rugby Oldfield.

A week later he played in the Reserves. He hobbled much better.

"How's it going?" asked Ben Robshaw, a Derby director.

"Alright. It's not a hundred per cent," Tim replied.

"Is it alright for the first team?"

"If selected."

On the afternoon of Thursday 21 April 1949, having played four first-team games in the previous fortnight, Tim visited his wife in the Queen Mary Nursing Home. He was told that the baby wasn't expected that night.

He went to bed, slept, got up, and answered the door to his mother-in-law. Tim put the kettle on, and it was still on when he arrived back three hours' later. The child, a boy, had been born at 6.30 in the morning, on the day before Derby County's 38th League game of the season. He weighed 7lb 15oz, and Derby won one-nil.

The Wards later celebrated by inviting everyone from the club to a party. The manager's wife brought an exquisite shawl which she had knitted herself. Raich Carter sent a book called *Year By Year: The Story of Our Baby.*

10. Football's Vera Lynns

Some of my father's mementoes were too alien for a small boy to understand. Take one of his programmes for instance – Combined Services CMF versus Combined Services BAOR at Trieste Stadium in Italy in the 1945-46 season. The programme is a single sheet of flimsy A4 paper, folded in the middle to produce four pages. It cost 10 lire.

It was all beyond my imagination. The game had taken place too far from home.

Despite regular changes of address during my schooldays, my mother dutifully kept all our mementoes, including Year by Year: The Story of Our Baby, *my birth present from Raich Carter. My mother was my first research assistant, the most formative, and the latent heroine of this tale. Thanks to her I can now reflect on my first birthday presents: a horse on wheels, a toy train, a humming top, plastic bricks, a tea set and various clothes. And I can study the details that my father diligently recorded in the workbook: the circumference of my head at birth (14in) and my age when I first crawled (10 months), stood (12 months), walked (15 months) and climbed (16 months).*

My parents always gave me enough freedom to find my own life, and, as an extra gift, they allowed me to discover theirs. I learned about their lives in a fragmented fashion; family revelations have no inherent logical order, and the events of football are rarely rational. Instead of a well-ordered chronological story, I was entertained by thematic tales, usually at meal-times or on quiet winter evenings. Eventually, I grew to understand what it meant when a footballer "missed the best years of his career to the war", and I grasped the meaning of missing an FA Cup Final.

1940

With a friend from his unit, Lofty Kerswill, Tim boarded a bus at one o'clock, ready to make his debut for yet another football club.

It was autumn, and Tim had been married for nine months. The Phoney War had given way to the Battle of Britain, then the Blitz. A furniture-remover had become a soldier in training, assigned to the 153 Field Ambulance Unit of the 15th Scottish Division and moved to Scotland.

Letters from Nancy showed that Derby was under bomb attack. Nancy, her sister Pat and her mother responded to sirens with a ritual. One ran upstairs to collect the tin-box of jewellery and insurance policies; then, together, they hurried across the road to the Co-op Bakery air-raid shelter. Inside the shelter they made futile attempts to sleep on a bench until the "all-clear" sounded. Finally they slept for an hour in their own beds before starting work.

Tim never sat still in the army. He trained all day, every day: an assault course, a "forced march" of 10 to 15 miles (running and walking against the clock) and then physical training exercises. But he wanted more, he craved football, so he asked around: "Where do they play football? What's the nearest club?" He found out, contacted the club, was made welcome, trained with their players, was chosen for the team, boarded the bus.

Tim and Lofty were in a good mood, until the Colonel got on the bus, followed by the Major.

"Best of luck this afternoon, Ward," said Major McNeill. "Put on a good show for the unit."

Tim could tell by the tone of his voice that the Major liked football. He relaxed.

"Do you want me to get you some tickets?" Tim asked.

"No, we've already arranged that. Why do you think you're playing?"

The bus made its short journey through Lanarkshire, from East Kilbride to Hamilton. The four men went to the match – one on the field and three in the stand – and all were satisfied when Hamilton Academicals beat Heart of Midlothian six-two and Tim scored a goal. The Hamilton manager, Mr McAndrew, gave Tim 50 shillings rather than the standard Scottish rate of two pounds (40 shillings).

"It'll cover your travel expenses," the friendly Scottish manager explained. So Tim and Lofty went to a restaurant in Cranfield Street and ate bacon, eggs, bread and butter to their total satisfaction. Money was no object.

"I'm coming up to Scotland in January," said England centre-forward Tommy Lawton.

"Tim's playing up here," said Scotland left-back Andy Beattie. "He'll fix you up with a game."

"Yes, certainly," said Tim, eager to oblige. "But you'll have to play well to get in our team."

Tim was teasing, but Hamilton did have a good centre-forward – Davie Wilson – who averaged more than a goal a game. When Hamilton beat Celtic one-nil, Tim had heard a Cadzow Street newspaper seller announcing the shock caused by big John Cassidy's goal: "Great fitba sensation, Davie Wilson didnae get his goal the day."

The three men talked on steps outside Ibrox Park in Glasgow. Tim had just played his first representative game, in front of the biggest crowd he had seen. He was the only Englishman in the Scottish Army team against the English Army and was confident enough among the international set. He knew his ground passing was now obsessionally accurate, and wondered if Stanley Rous had noticed. An international appearance next? Well, he was stationed only a few miles from Hampden. In wartime that might be enough.

"Where are you playing, Tim?" asked Tommy Lawton.

"Hamilton."

"Oh, that's alright. Can you fix me up with a game then?"

"I'll do my best. Which weekend is it?"

Tommy Lawton told him the date. The next morning, Tim spoke with the Hamilton manager: "Tommy Lawton is in Scotland on January the 18th. He's looking for a game. Can we fix him up with one?"

"Certainly," said McAndrew, obviously pleased.

1941

Tim went about training as usual. On Thursday 16 January, two days before Hamilton played at Greenock Morton, Tim checked the team list in the dressing-room. There was no sign of Tommy Lawton's name. "He must have cried off," Tim thought.

"Is Tommy not coming up then, Mr McAndrew?" Tim asked the Hamilton manager.

"Oh, yes. He's definitely coming." As Tim looked puzzled, Mr McAndrew continued. "He's playing for Morton."

"Morton?" queried Tim. "Why not us?"

"We'll get a better gate that way. The game's at Morton. If it had been at Hamilton we would have had him."

The manager was simply doing his wartime job. There was no promotion or relegation to worry about. It was recreation for players and spectators. So, on that Saturday, Tim was standing close to Tommy Lawton when the tall, sleek, black-haired England Adonis scored the first goal of the game – for Morton. Morton took a three-nil lead, but Hamilton pulled them back, the equaliser inevitably coming from Davie Wilson, with 15 minutes to play. After that, Morton attacked, Hamilton defended. At the end of the three-three draw, Tim shook hands with Tommy Lawton and they had a laugh together.

That was his last game for Hamilton Academicals. After playing in red-and-white hooped shirts in places like Paisley, Edinburgh and Falkirk, he was suddenly banished from the centrality of Hamilton, so near to Glasgow, so close to Hampden, within an illusion of playing for England. A train took his unit between the hills of Aberdeenshire, across the culture of Gibbon's *Sunset Song* to the awesome country of the Scottish Highlands. North, north, and further north. Tim's southern, rural, Gloucestershire upbringing was being left far behind. Football had schooled him in geography and the army was further education. His country was at war, his football-club employer had closed down and his wife was hundreds of miles away. At the tender age of 23, Tim Ward disappeared from his football family…for years rather than weeks.

1941 to 1943

He lived and worked in isolated camps near isolated towns. Near Lairg. Near Lybester. Near Thurso. And near Wick. Tim and his army colleagues were greeted by warm people in north of Scotland, people who had seen it all before: "Up here we have nine months of winter and three months of bad weather."

On some days they were thankful for six hours of light. They washed and shaved outdoors, and walked across duckboards to get to mobile baths. They were warmed by a ration of rum and braziers filled with coke. They ate a kipper at five and dreamed of a Saturday in Thurso (where there was little entertainment anyway). When the day's orders were complete, they entertained themselves with housey-housey.

Tim spent almost three years in northern Scotland. During that time, during fervent athletic years, through two-and-a-bit soccer seasons, he played six games of football with professional clubs and saw his wife four times.

1945

Kiel was one of Germany's most-bombed cities. It wasn't easy finding a decent football pitch there in August 1945. It was even harder finding a *stadium* with a passable pitch. The best had a bomb crater over one half. Soldiers worked hard to fill in the hole, the Nordmark Sports Palast was designated as a banqueting hall, and Derby County players arrived in time for lunch.

Tim was overjoyed to see them. The Colonel had assigned him a car and driver to bring him down from Travemunde, the Baltic town he had reached at the end of the war. Two lorry-loads of supporters came too. Now Tim explained to the Derby players that he was playing *against* them. He was in the Eighth Army team.

So what did these men talk about – the Derby County lads and the Eighth Army soldiers? Was it the assumed conversation of men, such as sport and sex, with a lot of swearing? Or, now the war in Europe was over, were there other matters to debate, like the future of the world?

The first topic was appearance. Tim, suntanned from working in good weather on the Lubecker Bucht, was ribbed about his skin colour, whereas the Derby lads were as "brown as cucumbers".

"I can see you've been lazing in the sun, Tim."

"We've been busy winning the war."

Leon Leuty, pale and wan from working nights at Rolls-Royce, was still shaken up from the journey to Germany.

"Tell them what happened, Leon," someone encouraged, so Leon told everyone about how the Derby County party had set off from Earls Colne in Essex in two RAF Halifax aeroplanes. Over Holland Leon thought he would explore the rear-gunner's turret. It took five minutes of contortion before he was installed in the seat. Then the pilot took the plane down to show passengers the flood damage caused when retreating Germans had destroyed dykes. Completely unexpectedly, the plane rose vertically like an express-lift. When Leon reappeared his face was as white as a goal-post. He thought the other lads had set him up for the trick but they claimed they were innocent. In fact the pilot had merely taken evasive action because the other plane was only a few feet away. Leon could laugh about it now, of course. He loved telling stories about his own misfortune, and this one took several minutes over lunch.

Leon told another story about himself, about the time he took a taxi from the centre of Derby and the fog was so thick along Osmaston Road that he got out and showed the driver the way by waving a handkerchief at the kerbside. When Leon reached his home he had walked most of the way, but he still paid the driver, later laughing infectiously as he told the story. He also had stories of gambling losses to tell a lunchtime crowd. It wasn't unknown for Leon to be seen in a telephone-kiosk 25 minutes before a game, placing a bet on a certain winner. He didn't take his own life too personally.

Sammy Crooks was with them. He looked the same as ever, still as thin as a lath. He never put on weight, always told stories. A few days before, the Derby players had been taken towards Denmark, where they visited a Russian canteen and were treated to vodka. One sip nearly knocked off Leon's head. When Sammy tried it, he began hiccoughing, and he hiccoughed through the next two days. Then, when they were dissuaded from visiting a place with two cases of typhus, Sammy quickly remarked that he and the lads would soon sup their way through those cases too.

Whatever they talked about, these men savoured football analogies – "Think of the win bonus for winning this war, lads" – and used swear words. Did they swear every 10th word, every 30th, every 100th? Tim was unusual in that he rarely swore. He was still swayed by the gentlemanly spirit in life, the acceptance that others have better breeding. He aspired to such people.

The players teased each other about the game ahead: the Eighth Army lads said how much fitter they were, how the crowd was on their side and how the bombed pitch would be in their favour; the Derby County players said how well they had been playing and how they had scored ten in the first game of the tour.

What else did they talk about? It was three weeks since Clement Attlee had won the General Election for Labour, against the run of play, so to speak, so did they talk about politics? Footballers didn't normally – it might be too disruptive to team spirit – but this was something special. Tim had voted Labour in that election, a unique cross in his life. If they didn't talk about that election, they would certainly have mentioned football politics. Sammy Crooks, national representative for the Players' Union, was busy negotiating players' wages and contracts. Some trouble was ahead.

At the Kilia Sports Ground that afternoon, most of the spectators, 5,000-6,000 of them, wore uniform. Some were Royal Air Force, some Royal Navy, the majority Army. The Eighth Army were playing at home. Comments from the crowd reinforced it.

"I hope you get a low demob number," shouted one spectator after a mistake by an Eighth Army player.

After the Eighth Army's one-nil win, after the post-match banquet, after speeches by Derby chairman Ben Robshaw, manager Ted Magner and senior professional Sammy Crooks, Tim said enforced goodbyes and returned to his unit. The army paid his money, Derby County waited for his demobilisation. His high demob number – Group 28 – suggested he would be released around Christmas, just in time for the FA Cup games of 1946.

Two days later Tim heard news that might speed up his release. He relayed it to his Colonel, who had sent for him on another matter.

"The Japanese have capitulated," Tim said.

"Is that right?"

"Yes."
"Thank God," said the Colonel.

Tim looked down the wing. It was no ordinary left wing, with Dally Duncan at the other end of a quick glance, but the wing of a light aircraft. His first experience of flying approached a terrifying climax. Fog concealed the airport at Bückeburg.

"There's no need to go down here," said the Canadian pilot. "We can take you to Brussels and fix you up with a weekend there."

"Well, we'd like to play," said Tim, who knew that a vehicle was waiting to drive them from Bückeburg to Düsseldorf. Then he heard the plane brush against branches of tall trees as the pilot went in for a closer look.

The other passenger in the plane was Everton's Albert Johnson. The two footballers were thrilled to have received a message to report to Flensburg by special driver and jeep. At Flensburg they boarded a plane arranged by Major Tomlinson, who was in charge of a soccer team formed to represent the British Army of the Rhine (BAOR), itself newly-formed after the relocation of so many British troops. (The 15th Scottish soldiers called it the "British Army *over* the Rhine" to emphasise their early crossing.)

Aboard the light aircraft, hovering over Bückeburg, Tim Ward and Albert Johnson were not enjoying the ride. They were soon convinced that the pilot was right. They should fly on to Brussels.

They landed safely at Brussels, and travelled north-east to Düsseldorf by 15-cwt truck with Eddie Hapgood and Billy Hughes, who were playing for BAOR the next day. The four players arrived at a stadium in Düsseldorf just as a practice game entered its last 20 minutes.

"You've made a great effort just to land in Brussels with all the theatres of war going on," said Major Tomlinson. "And a lot of people would have stayed in Brussels. You must be mad!"

The next day Tim travelled with the BAOR team to Cologne, where he played his début for yet another new team in front of 35,000 people. They lost five-two to Notts County, but he scored a goal, as he had on his débuts for Charlton Kings, Cheltenham Town first team, Derby County "A", Hamilton Academicals and the Scottish Army XI.

On returning to his unit he accepted the fateful mood that had dominated his football career – don't call us, we'll call you – and resigned himself to not hearing any more from Major Tomlinson. Instead he was soon told to report to Wuppertal, where a squad of 16 or 17 BAOR players trained like a professional club. It was an ever-changing squad, some players leaving when they were demobbed, others joining. When Tim arrived, he knew he had a Group-28 demob listing, and he expected he would be among the last to leave. "Certainly no later than January," he thought.

He was soon playing regularly for the BAOR team, one or two games a week against the best teams in Europe, and he began to enjoy himself. His life was no longer in danger, he was back among professional footballers and playing in front of large crowds. The spectators were friendly. As servicemen they supported

BAOR; as loyal supporters they sometimes supported opponents. When faced with conflicting loyalties, most of them simply supported both teams and cheered and clapped any good play.

It was like being on tour with an England team: spoiled with good facilities, representing millions and being presented to dignitaries before the games. Dressed in red shirts and blue shorts, they entertained the troops. They were the Vera Lynns of the footballing world.

Tim knew he was part of a great team when they played Glasgow Rangers in Hanover. Thirty thousand spectators, soldiers and airmen (no Germans allowed), wedged themselves into the stadium, the pipers of the Sixth Battalion Seaforths played to the crowd, and even the Celtic supporters were pleased to see Rangers. That was especially so when the goals went into the Rangers net and trainer Arthur Dixon held his head in his hands in a picture of misery.

BAOR six, Glasgow Rangers one.

After the stadium was cleared, flocks of Germans moved in to collect discarded cigarette ends.

During the next fortnight, two more British club teams were beaten with relative ease.

BAOR four, Nottingham Forest one.

BAOR three, Queen's Park nil.

After defeat to an FA XI, which included Leon Leuty, in Düsseldorf, they moved on to Münster, where they were visited by one of the best club sides in England at the time. They should have won more easily than they did.

BAOR two, Birmingham nil.

"Hey, this is international stuff," Tim thought. "This is a great team."

Over friendly meals, on visits to the theatre or the cinema, or when they were together on army transport going to the stadium, they talked with opponents about developments in Britain or about harrowing journeys from Britain to Germany. Most of his opponents had made their aircraft débuts and were still recovering. Most faced eventful trips home. The Nottingham Forest team's aeroplane was diverted from Syerston to Margate in a gale. Birmingham players were held up by fog and three Welsh internationals were worried that they might miss the Scotland match. Fog also delayed the return of Queen's Park, the Scottish amateur team. Their reserve team had to fulfil a fixture against Queen of the South on the Saturday.

"To hell with the Russkies," said the Canadian pilot as he steered his Dakota through the Berlin Blockade, escorted by two American "Lightnings".

The BAOR players were travelling from Berlin to Warsaw, one half of the team looking across the inside of the plane at the other half – until they were tossed about too much to look anywhere. They arrived in Warsaw on a snowy Saturday. It was just like a real match day, except that before the game they were taken to the Warsaw ghetto where large numbers of Jews had been killed.

They drew the first game against a Polish international team, and played another the following day. By this time the snow had turned to rain. Two minutes from the end they were drawing again, and Dennis Westcott attacked through the centre for the BAOR team. A defender tackled clumsily and Westcott tumbled over into the snow. The referee gave a penalty.

Dave Russell was captain that day, even though he didn't live at Wuppertal with the other BAOR players. Russell was in the RAF, brought into the team on occasions when Wing-Commander Adams – rather than Major Tomlinson – was in charge. Russell knew the regular BAOR penalty-taker was Les Compton, so had a word with him, remarking on the wartime friendship between the British and the Poles, saying how much the Poles had been through.

"Perhaps I had better take it myself," said Dave Russell.

He picked up the ball, placed it on the penalty spot and walked back to the edge of the penalty area.

"Is he going to miss this penalty?" Tim wondered, but he never got to find out.

As Russell walked away from the penalty spot, facing his own goal, Reg Lewis of Arsenal ran surreptitiously towards the ball and kicked it into the net. As Lewis walked past Tim, he shook his head and muttered to himself: "Bloody miss a penalty. What's the world coming to? Bloody miss a penalty . . ."

Finally, Tim got to play against Scotland. There were two fixtures in two days, and he played in the first. The BAOR team lost that game, four-two, in a stadium in the tiny town of Celle that overflowed with 10,000 people, but they drew one-one in Hamburg the following day.

In Hamburg, the crowd began arriving three and a half hours before kick-off, and there were 40,000 of them when the game started. Some of them had hitchhiked huge distances, and scores broke into the stand and occupied seats reserved for officials.

Field Marshal Montgomery appeared in the dressing-room after the game. He told the players that his seat was one of those occupied before the game.

"I wouldn't have minded," he said. "But it was Private in the Pioneer Corps."

"Put on a good show," said Montgomery. "Win all your games. I'll expect a daily report on the team's progress."

He asked if they were being looked after.

"We've only got one problem," said one of Tim's team-mates. "Some of us can't get into the Officer's Mess after a game."

Without hesitation, Montgomery made the necessary promotions. Corporal Ward was promoted to Sergeant. It was the first major honour of his football career.

Stan Cullis met them in Italy. Stan Cullis of Wolverhampton Wanderers and England. Sergeant-Major Cullis of the British Army.

"I better warn you, lads," Stan said. "Colonel Cox has an aversion to footballers."

They were given huts to share with other servicemen, a real contrast to Wuppertal, where they had good billets and could stay in bed as long as they wanted to.

At 6.30 on the first morning they were woken up by reveille. An Italian shouted something to do with being out on parade.

"What's going on?" a footballer muttered.

"Bugger off," another one advised in imperfect Italian.

"No, no," the Italian replied. And that's when a dozen football boots flew through the air and hit him somewhere around the bugle.

Major Tomlinson came down to sort it out, and within 24 hours there was an apology from General Ritchie.

After the trip to Italy and Austria – five games (four wins and a draw) in 17 days and first sight of Tom Finney ("This lad's got the makings of a player") – the BAOR players were given Christmas leave. They were told to come back when they were ready. An open pass. "Don't be too greedy," Major Tomlinson said, so the players met and agreed on a fortnight's leave. In those 14 days, Tim played five games of football for Derby County, including the first leg of the third-round FA Cup game. He was playing better than ever.

1946

The BAOR roadshow continued to roll through European countryside with midweek matches against British club sides. On Saturdays and Sundays they played other representative teams. Cliff Michelmore and Alan Clarke commentated on games, and a word from one of the footballers would often ensure a request was played: " and now...*crackle, crackle*...for the boys of the BAOR soccer team...*crackle, crackle*...*Temptations* by Perry Como."

An hour's time difference between Britain and the rest of Europe meant the BAOR team could finish a midweek or Saturday game and then return in time to tune in to the World Service and hear the tail-end of Raymond Glendenning's football commentary from Britain.

It was an odd letter from Nancy. A cryptic letter. It needed to get past the censor. Derby County manager Stuart McMillan had invited Nancy to the Baseball Ground and talked to her. That was clear enough. But there was something else in the letter, something about a Colonel doing some work on Tim's demobilisation.

Tim knew Derby County wanted him home quickly. McMillan had hinted as much when he was home at Christmas.

Tim wrote back to Nancy to say he didn't think Major Tomlinson would release him. He wondered if he should try to pull strings. He tried unsuccessfully to see Philip Noel-Baker, his Member of Parliament, who was touring the Continent. He didn't know what was happening. He wasn't sure what to do.

Nancy also told him about Derby County's fourth-round tie with West Bromwich. The Baseball Ground was full for the home leg, and people were standing on top of the grandstand. The away game was played in a blizzard. Derby County had won of course. They were through to the fifth round.

Training was more fun than it had ever been – five-a-sides and head tennis in the morning, billiards or a walk in the afternoon. George Swindin put them through exercises, and the players reacted conscientiously.

Tim knew that Derby County had a good set of experienced players back in England – Raich Carter, Peter Doherty, Sammy Crooks, Jack Nicholas and Dally Duncan – but he felt that he was training and playing with the *next* generation of international players. Some of his BAOR colleagues, like Les Compton (Arsenal), Billy Hughes (Birmingham) and Dennis Westcott (Wolves), had already played for their countries. Others, like Reg Lewis (Arsenal), Billy Steel (Greenock Morton), Eddie Baily (Tottenham), Alex Ormston (Stoke) and Eric Parsons (West Ham) were expected to play for their countries soon. Most were in their twenties. Most were tipped for big futures. Tim was proud to be with them. "This can only help my career," he thought.

Older soldiers had been demobilised first. The younger ones had been the first to enlist, and now looked like being the last back to Britain. It made some sense, as younger ones were less likely to have jobs and families waiting for them. But it made little sense to Tim. He had a job and a wife to go back to.

Tim hung around the Arsenal players and learned what he could. He learned a new trick from Reg Lewis. Lewis called it the "Alex James stutter" and claimed to have learned it from the Scottish maestro. Tim saw Reg Lewis beat three men with the trick, so he practised hard. To a player running alongside it gives the impression that the man with the ball is slowing down and changing direction, causing a marker to hesitate for a moment while the player with the ball runs on to gain an extra yard or two of space.

At night they slept in billets in the stadium at Wuppertal. Major Tomlinson was in barracks at Osnabrück, over 80 miles away. Even when he wasn't there, he made sure the players were looked after very well. There were cars at the stadium, with drivers waiting to take them where they wanted. There was even a plane standing by for the longer journeys to games.

They came out of the Wuppertal stadium to go half a mile into town. They had just watched the film again, for the second time that week. Someone had found the film in the bowels of the stadium, and Tim assumed it had been confiscated by Germans at the start of the war. The film showed the 1936 Olympics, not only Jesse Owens winning his races but also Adolf Hitler storming out of the stadium. It must have been made by an American or a Briton. The BAOR players couldn't watch it enough.

"Shall we take the suspension railway to town?"

"We can walk in, surely?"

"No," said Reg Lewis. "We've got a plane, haven't we?"

They all laughed with relief. They'd come some distance from sleepless nights in fields, although there was still a long way to go. There were Tim's rigors, for instance.

Another letter from Nancy. Even more cryptic. She had been to the Baseball Ground again but Stuart McMillan was not having much luck. He wanted her to go to her doctor and get Tim home on compassionate grounds. There was something in the letter about "Nancy's nerves". She also said she had never felt fitter.

The Rams beat Brighton, she wrote. *We are into the sixth round. All the factories switched their hours round. Workers were given the afternoon off to see the game. The ground was full again.*

Münster transit camp. Saturday morning. A collection of regular visitors, the BAOR footballers, ate breakfast and talked about their abortive trip to Berlin. They had arrived on the Saturday expecting to play Moscow Dynamo the next day, but the

Dynamo team had gone back to Moscow. The BAOR players trained at the Olympic Stadium. That was a new experience.

The transit camp was a place to meet people they knew, a place were they enjoyed talking football. The RSM was a friend of the players. He always came in to have a chat. He always fixed up an extra ration of cigarettes for them. Cigarettes were currency. The Germans worshipped them like they had once worshipped Hitler.

Les Compton was concerned about a bet he had placed on Derby County when their odds for the FA Cup were 10-1, but Tim was reassuring – "It's alright, Les, we'll walk it" – and hoped for a sixth-round victory over Aston Villa, who had been Cup favourites in January.

Like most camps, Münster had a team playing in a service league. The camp's RSM crept up to the BAOR boys with unusual diffidence.

"We were wondering if one or two of you lads fancied a game this afternoon," he said. "We haven't won a game yet, and we're playing the top of the league. It would be nice if we didn't get beat by too many."

"We'll all play," somebody ventured.

The RSM looked a little embarrassed.

"Well, our PTI will have to play."

"Ten of us'll play then."

So ten BAOR players and one Physical Training Instructor turned out in a Service league game. It was a good time to experiment with playing in different positions.

After the 18th goal went in, the opposition looked bemused. One of them spoke aloud: "Some of you lads can play a bit. Who's that big centre-forward?"

"Ever heard of Leslie Compton?"

"Yeah. He played for the Arsenal."

"That's him."

After the game the Münster RSM was even more embarrassed. "I think I might get into trouble," he said.

Tim listened to the wireless as soon as he could.

Derby County hung on to beat Aston Villa on aggregate.

And went through to the semi-final.

The last four of the FA Cup.

They were doing well without him.

Portsmouth came out to play them at Hanover, and the BAOR lads talked to the players about another delayed journey, the Bolton Disaster and the FA Cup. Portsmouth still held the FA Cup. They had won it in 1939 and kept it for nearly seven years, only recently handing it back. The trophy had been lucky to survive the war. It escaped a bomb only because the manager had the foresight to take it home to his cellar rather than leave it in the bank (which was hit later the same night).

There was one other thing the players talked about – the cold.

It was a real winter. A deep covering of snow was removed from the Hindenburg stadium pitch by volunteers, and there was no hot water in the dressing-rooms. Amazingly, 20,000 people braved the cold to see the game.

BAOR three, Portsmouth one.

The Portsmouth party then won the prize for "worst return trip". Flying conditions were unsuitable, so they travelled overland. They spent 17 hours in an Army lorry, careering over bomb-torn roads in bitterly cold weather, then 16 hours in a train, before they arrived at Calais for a boat trip across the channel.

The next visitors made an easier trip but were faced with similar difficulties on the pitch.

BAOR two, Manchester United one.

Everton were the next opponents for the BAOR team. Players from both teams were taken on a coach outing and shown the damage to the Möhne and Eder dams. The players chatted amicably.

"Who do you fancy in the semi-final replay?" Tim asked Joe Mercer, the Everton and England captain. "Derby or Birmingham?"

"You must fancy Derby," Joe replied. "I picked up the paper on Sunday and saw that Carter and Doherty hadn't played well. Those buggers couldn't play bad in *two* matches."

That Wednesday, after Everton had beaten BAOR three-two, Tim listened to the wireless commentary on the semi-final replay. The enormity of the event struck him for the first time. A crowd of what? Did he say over *eighty* thousand? And people being moved back so that corner-kicks and throw-ins could be taken.

Tim heard the game go into extra-time. The reception was never very good. What did he say? What was that? Who scored that goal? He stuck the story together, piece by piece.

Birmingham nil, Derby County four.

The Rams were through to the Cup Final. Against Charlton Athletic. At Wembley.

BAOR won again. Beat Wolves three-one. Ray Harrison came in laughing. "A bit odd really," Tim thought, as Ray had missed a simple chance near the end.

"What's funny, Ray?" someone asked.

"Oh, one I hadn't heard before." Ray Harrison explained. "You know, when I missed that chance at the end, and I finished at the back of the goal."

"Yeah."

"Someone shouted out, 'Harrison, why don't you wipe your bloody glasses.'"

They all laughed.

None of them wore glasses.

11.
Homecoming Truths

I walked into the kitchen and sensed something different. Breakfast was mushrooms on toast. A special treat. Something was afoot.

"Andrew, we want you to help us make a decision," my father said. "You see, I've been offered the job at Derby County."

"The job" meant manager. That much was understood.

The mushrooms on toast arrived. My favourite food. Yet my father's news cost me a moment's hesitation. No more than a moment.

As I ate, my father talked some more: "It doesn't matter either way to us ...I know you've made friends here in Grimsby and Cleethorpes...You might not want to leave them."

I tucked into the mushrooms.

Give my mother credit. I might not have eaten anything but my favourite.

"Derby haven't got a very good team," I said. "And I like our colours better."

I thought of our daring red shorts, and our fight with the Football League to become the first team to wear them. But "our" had a transient meaning in professional football. I knew that. We'd moved before.

"The team's my problem," said my father. He spoke confidently. What with his team-selection and my horseshoe-rubbing, Derby County were almost guaranteed promotion. "Grimsby's a two-year job really," he said.

"A two-year job?" I asked.

"Managers come and go from here...it's out of the way...a bit of a dead-end...they've a big board of directors...it's not a job where managers stop for very long."

"Any more mushrooms, Mum? Please?"

"Derby are offering me a contract...I've never had a contract before...and this one's for five years...you won't have to change schools again...but we're happy to leave the decision up to you."

I concentrated on breakfast. I was making a good job of the mushrooms, but my father's next comment distracted me.

"You'd be able to watch some county cricket in Derby," he said.

I looked up, smiled, gazed smugly out of the window.

"You can think about it," my father continued. "Hurry along now, or you'll be late for school."

I was too well-trained to tell my school-mates the news until my father gave me the word, but I probably already knew that we were leaving Grimsby. Not because I wanted a glimpse of county cricket. No, there was something else. The words "Derby County" were special in our family. I had met some of my parents' memories already, passed on in a vague and spurious way, but I knew there were more to come if we returned to the source.

We were stopped on Derby's main street.

"Hello, Tim," said the man, shaking my father's hand. "This is Tim Ward," he told the son at his side. "I've told you about him."

My father shook hands with a boy of seven or eight.

A few more friendly words, then the man walked away with his son.

"Who was that, Dad?" I asked.

"I haven't a clue," he replied. "I've never seen him before."

"Oh," I said.

My father hadn't seemed fazed, but it seemed odd to me.

What had happened in Derby, the town where I was born? What kind of a club were Derby County? Where was he during the war? And why didn't he play in that 1946 FA Cup Final if he was an international player?

I had no real answers to these questions.

Until now.

My childhood immersed me in a volatile sporting world which offered pleasure and pain, help and hindrance. It could be cruel, baffling, uplifting, dominating, energising, but it was rarely boring. Excitement was inevitable. In the routine way that families ate Cornflakes or watched Coronation Street *on television, we wondered what would happen on Saturdays. I grew up thinking that work had to be interesting and enjoyable with well-defined measures of success and a journey into the unknown every season.*

"What will you do when you grow up?"

"Play football of course…or cricket."

I played for school cricket teams from the under-13s upwards, but my football skills did not develop until later, when I found more confidence. Even when young, I was wary that someone might approach me in the street and speak those crushing words: "You'll never be as good as your father."

When I was 17, and playing well for my school team, Peter Doherty and Andy Beattie called at our house. My father thought his old friends had come to see him. *Instead they wanted me to sign as an amateur for Notts County. Shortly after that, three things happened: my father lost his job as manager of Derby County; we moved to Carlisle; and I concentrated harder on my studies. I played for Penrith in the Northern League – one full game and once as a substitute – and then other things interfered. I didn't have my father's ambition and desire for competition. More than anything, I didn't have his talent. I had grown up at the wrong end of a football ground, with too much security and without older brothers to aspire to.*

Before I leave my football career, however, let me tell you about some sweet moments from one season in my late twenties. My father, then 60, was playing regularly for a team in the Burton and District Sunday League, and he talked me into playing. He was on the left side of midfield and I was wide on the left. I have an abiding image from that season of him hunched over the ball, jogging forward, nudging the ball from foot to foot, his body swaying inside and out, waiting for the perfect moment to pass the ball into my path, precisely into my stride, with the inside of his right foot or the outside of his left. The strength and direction of those passes were professionally conceived, perfectly weighted, and suddenly I was Johnny McCann, Dally Duncan, Raich Carter, Tom Finney and Stan Matthews in a shared experience that didn't have to be spoken about. I didn't need anything more from my football career. I could retire happily at least 10 years before my father did from his.

1946

He travelled home to England on the Wednesday before the Cup Final – to York, where he was formally demobilised at Fulford Barracks. He exchanged his army kit for a trilby hat and civilian suit. The suits came in two colours – a wide blue stripe or grey – but Tim knew that, whichever he chose, the double-breasted style would make him look like a Chicago gangster come to steal Cup-Final tickets.

Wearing his new outfit, a booklet in his pocket ("For Your Guidance: What To Do on Leaving the Service, and How To Do It"), he travelled home to Derby. At the railway station he met the Cup Final buzz head on. Passengers, railway workers and newspapers carried the latest news. One newspaper seller – called Sam but known as "Bread and Jam" – was small, bespectacled and witty, if repetitive at times. During the war he wrote his own placards, shouting revelations to the Derby public: "Germans in Berlin," "Snow in Moscow." He also knew the Derby public's love of football. "Match edition," he shouted. "Read all about it…Rams team announced…and what a bloody team."

Tim read the *Derby Evening Telegraph* and talked to people about the news. Derby County's Cup Final team had been chosen on the Monday.

During the war, Tim had always been able to come home on leave and get a game. It was different this time. This time there was no game for him.

He soon learned that £1 Cup Final tickets were going for a fiver on the established black market, and three-and-sixpenny ones for anything up to three pounds. A bottle of gin might help strike a deal, but only if there was a spare ticket.

"You'll be lucky, mate," people said. "You can't get one for love or money."

He knew he hadn't got a place in the team. Now he wondered if he had a place in the crowd.

Tim arrived at his mother-in-law's about 8pm. The entire family were there. He took off his trilby, threw it through the doorway and awaited the fun. The greetings came thick and fast. The trilby was bent into all shapes and used as a football. Tim never wore it again. If the family were short of a cheap laugh, they could bring out the hat.

On Thursday Tim reported for work at the Baseball Ground. He was given full-time employment on £10 a week. In one way he was lucky, as many soldiers had to search for work, those still alive and fit enough to work. On the other hand he was unlucky. Hadn't he gone away as a first-team player? And what was he now?

The Baseball Ground was an odd environment. The first-team were staying at Harpenden in Hertfordshire, where they were presumed to be training, playing golf and taking trips to the London theatre. There was no sign of reserve-team players either. They had played at Sheffield Wednesday the previous night and were given the day off.

The club was in chaos. No players. Just a few hard-working officials trying to satisfy the demand for tickets, and supporters unsuccessfully trying to barter for tickets with black-market carpets or legs of ham. Tim was given two complimentary tickets and allowed to buy two more. He gave one to Nancy's Uncle Charlie.

The next Monday, two days after Derby County had won the FA Cup Final, Tim went through his habitual changing routine in the away-team dressing-room at the Dell, home of Southampton Football Club. He pulled on the white shirt of Derby County and those familiar black-and-white socks. His boots had been kept by Derby County for seven years, stored under "21", the number he had been given when he arrived at the club. The last part of his ritual was to put on shorts. Black shorts. He was back doing what he wanted to do all his life. Playing professional football. Playing for Derby County.

Yet something didn't seem right. Eight of his colleagues had Cup-winners medals, won two days previously. Tim did not. Nor did Dave McCulloch, in for Raich Carter, or Angus Morrison, wearing "11" in place of Dally Duncan.

On the field, lining up at left-half, replacing Chick Musson, Tim looked around at his team-mates and wondered if he was one of the few concentrating. Eleven minutes later, with Derby two-nil behind, he had extra cause to think. His colleagues' celebratory season was almost over, his own English season just beginning. While he was in the dressing-room at half-time, the Cup was paraded around the Southampton ground. It seemed appropriate that he was distanced from it.

After the game – Derby lost four-two – the Cup was taken to a Southampton hotel. He knew that the next day the whole of Derby would turn out to welcome them. But it was the Cup-winning players they would want to see, not the soldier who was home from the war. He felt like a spectator who had strayed into a penalty area while a penalty kick was being taken.

They travelled home on Tuesday. Home to Derby with the FA Cup. A beer-dray awaited them at Shardlow, a few miles outside Derby. It was an eight-ton beer-dray, supplemented by the head of a dead ram, supplied by a local butcher and worth a lot of ration coupons.

One by one, at seven o'clock that Tuesday evening, the Derby County players came down the steps of their long-distance bus and on to the open-top beer-dray.

All except Tim.

He stayed on the coach, not sure what to do. No one asked him if he was joining the others on the beer-dray, and he started to feel estranged from the Cup-winning team. He was left alone with a bus-driver, while other Derby County players prepared for a celebratory drive through Derby streets to Police Headquarters, where there was a suitable balcony for the players to be welcomed by the crowd before going to the nearby Council Houses for a more formal reception.

For spectators, waiting for a view of their heroes, waiting for a sight of the FA Cup, it was like being on the terraces. Hemmed in, desperate for a better view, they persevered happily through the customary boredom of waiting. The entertainment did not last 120 minutes this time, or even 90, but perhaps just a few seconds, just long enough to see the Cup and the players. Britain had waited seven years for a Cup Final. Derby had waited more than fifty for the Rams to win the Cup. What was a few more minutes of hanging around?

It wasn't a colourful sight, it was a black-and-white sight: people dressed in drab make-do-and-mend wartime clothing or demob suits. They displayed black-and-white rosettes, swinging rattles, flying hats and caps, large and small banners, kites and confetti. They had saved their wastepaper, eaten their scraps, dug for victory and cooked what they could from parsnips. Now they were really celebrating. People stood on chairs to see the carnival procession. The streets were a mass of people, one body of enthusiasm. It was too much for some – they fainted.

On the beer-dray, the players signed autographs. A supporter jumped on to shake Jack Nicholas's hand. He jumped off again, shaking his own. The players were overwhelmed, although Raich Carter had known such celebrations before. Raich looked smart and sober, dressed in a suit with a white handkerchief bobbing out of his breast pocket. He might have been remembering the Sunderland Cup-winning reception of 1937, the noise of ships' hooters, railway engines' whistles and thousands of people singing "Blaydon Races". Near to Raich, trainer Dave Willis lit a cigarette.

Tim, still the lone passenger on the coach that followed the beer-dray, saw less and less of the Derby County players as the crowd blocked the road. He was concerned with the pressure of people on the sides of his vehicle. A procession of cars, bicycles and pedestrians tried to follow the beer-dray. Tim's bus-driver could not drive through the throng with safety.

"You should have been out there," someone shouted, recognising Tim.

There were thousands outside, and yet Tim was alone on his bus, alone and feeling lonely. He recognised a supporter he knew and invited him on to the coach, then another and another. Soon there were five or six for company. People talked to him.

"Where've you been?"

"I've been away at the war," he replied.

"When were you demobbed?"

"Last Wednesday."

"That's late, isn't it?"

"I must have been too valuable."

"You've been fighting for your country. You think they'd let you fight for your town."

The bus was stuck, wedged in by the crowd. The gap between the beer-dray and Tim's bus increased. Tim watched the top of the beer-dray as the other vehicle moved forward towards its destination.

Crowds of screaming, cheering people, and none of it for him. And yet he had felt a hero in the rest of Europe, playing to huge audiences for what he felt was an even greater team, a representative team rather than a club team. In his eyes, the excitement, privilege and friendliness of BAOR soccer was more limelit than Derby County's Cup run. Yet, at that moment, in one of the greatest moment's in the town's history, no one wanted him. It was as though some other club had won the Cup. Not his club.

He got off his bus and started walking.

He heard cheers, erratic and tumultuous, and presumed the players were appearing in front of the crowd. One by one, with the FA Cup. They could probably hear the cheers in Nottingham. He heard someone say it must be the biggest event in the history of the town. He heard it, but he walked in the opposite direction.

As he took his confused, solitary walk away from the cheering thousands, towards the house his wife had bought in Arnold Street, he fought hard not to feel bitter about losing seven years of his career to the war. He tried to deny that success was bypassing him in his adopted town. He recognised that club officials had other things to think about than him. He would remind himself that Derby County had been good to him.

What did it matter that he had missed one game that happened to be at Wembley? Derby County had provided him with the boyhood satisfaction of identifying with a team capable of beating Cedric's Arsenal. They had rescued him from Lindner's factory, paid him good wages for two-and-a-half years of full-time football, offered him a chance of winning a League Championship medal in 1938-39 and provided him with a surrogate family of brothers. Then, during the interruption of a bloody war, they had helped him again. They had kept his job waiting for him and given him games of football when he came home on leave. And they had presented him with a talisman that had saved his sanity in Europe. They had armed him with a football.

Postscript

When my mother had a stroke, in December 1992, and my father went into hospital with only a few weeks to live, I moved a few clothes and a computer to their home in Staffordshire and settled in. In the next few weeks I was astounded by the support I received, especially from the world of professional football.

At my father's funeral, a great phalanx of strength stood behind me like a Kop waiting to carry our family through a game. Apparently someone looked around and said, "You could pick a great team from those here today."

After his death, my mother moved to a residential home. I know I have said little about my mother in this book, even though, along the way, I collected my mother's memories too. I have simply chosen not to publish her story in the same detail as my father's, because this book is about a particular relationship – father and son and football.

As my mother settled into her new home, I had the job of clearing out the family cottage. I knew my father very well, but bereaved houses always have emotional crevasses. There were wartime love letters to my mother, letters from famous people in football and supportive letters from a Member of Parliament after my father had lost his job as manager of Derby County in 1967. His 1959-60 Football Association diary contained entries that sandwiched his duties as football manager and father: Cup tickets on sale at Oakwell; Founders' Day at Wakefield Grammar School in the Cathedral; and Sheffield Wednesday v Torpedo of Moscow.

There were mementoes that charted his football career – a silver medal for winning the Cheltenham and District League Division Four, a Nazi flag captured in 1945, a pennant from Antwerp in 1946, a violin and doll from Czechoslovakia later that same year, three England international caps (one for an FA tour of Canada in 1950), blazer buttons with England lions on them, a 1950 Charity Shield plaque, a Festival of Britain miner's lamp, a silver tankard from the supporters club at Barnsley, a silver salver to commemorate Grimsby Town's promotion in 1961-62, a Dukla Prague pennant, the Ansell's Charity Cup won by his ex-Rams team, ties with football-club crests, a rabbit's foot in a bedside drawer and shoes that were worn down at the back in such a way that they could only have belonged to a footballer with good balance. There were also his war medals. He had laughed about them. He had sent off for them in 1979 and had received the wrong ones.

While clearing out the house, I also found an old manuscript of mine. It was the first draft of this book, written as a more conventional biography, covering my father's life from his birth in 1917 to his 70th birthday. It ended by describing a visit he had made to the Baseball Ground to talk to a group of older Derby County supporters. He went with Kevin Hector, a great favourite, not only with Derby County fans but also with my father. At the end of their talk, there was an opportunity for the audience to ask questions. A man stood up. "I don't want to ask a question," he said. "I just want to make an observation. I would have given my right arm to have been a professional footballer, but I wasn't good enough. I would give anything now to have memories like yours." When the man sat down he was visibly moved.

My manuscript gave the basic outline of this story. In the margin, my father had written these words: "When he sat down the man was in tears and so was I. I noticed that Kevin had gone very quiet. As I drove slowly home afterwards I could not help but think of the man's admission and I thought how lucky I had been. To play football in 20 different countries; to be paid a good salary to keep myself fit; to have travelled extensively; to have stayed at the very best of hotels; to have survived everything a war can do to you; and, above all, to have been British."

Finally, when I was through with packing boxes, I sat in the family home and experienced the emptiness. I stopped at each room and let the images storm in. Upstairs I looked in the box-room, where, in a fit of energy one night in 1976, I had banged away at a typewriter in my first attempt to write something about my father's experiences. I looked in my bedroom, where I had studied during university vacations, books resting unsteadily on a folding table, body wrapped in warm clothing in the days before my parents had considered central heating. Downstairs, in the lounge, the strongest image was of half a dozen people sitting around as my father told a story from the past, my mother happy in the jollity, occasionally prompting with a few words: "Tell them the sago pudding story, Tim." In the kitchen the three of us had eaten and talked at very regular times, and new stories had unfolded and I had reached for a note-book. And the living-room was where my father and I had sat in old uncomfortable chairs while he reminisced and my mother and I listened.

During the difficult period after his death, I had great support from the next-door neighbours, Sally and Bob, and I came to realise that Sally's children, Rachell and Stuart, had also claimed a part in my parents' lives. Stuart played football with my father for hours, kicking a ball back and forth across the garden, my father teasing him with controlled flicks and kicks that had improved steadily for over 70 years.

Isn't it funny how a four-year-old boy can make a 74-year-old man happy in the spring before his death? All it needed was a ball and a few precious words: "Can Tim come out to play?" All it needed was a football and a friend.